CHALK DUST AND CHEWING GUM

Mrs Bream's return to teaching after twenty years was unpremeditated, almost accidental – but after the first tentative step it was practically impossible to draw back. Although a graduate and teacher-trained before marriage, she had no previous experience, but now, as a mature person, she found herself in the blackboard jungle of a city school, with a class of low-ability children under her care.

With warmth, sympathy and humour Mrs Bream brings to life her superficially worldly-wise, amoral, lazy, unscrupulous and often dirty pupils, who emerge as entertaining, lively and often delightful individuals.

But above all her book shows the actual business of teaching – its problems, its agonies, its compensations, its truly vocational aspect – with a vividness which will strike a chord with every teacher – and will go far in helping parents understand what a tough job teaching is.

There is food for thought in this book, savoured with a humour and kindliness that makes for most entertaining reading.

CHALK
DUST
AND
CHEWING
GUM

Freda Bream

Collins

AUCKLAND AND LONDON

First published 1970
Collins Bros. & Co., Ltd.
P. O. Box No. 1, Auckland

Printed in Hong Kong by
Dai Nippon Printing Co., (International) Ltd.

Chapter 1

I returned from the local shops that afternoon to find a tall, scholarly-looking gentleman standing on my back porch. This was unusual. Scholarly-looking gentlemen did not normally grace my back porch. Small boys, yes. And scraps of paper and the neighbour's ginger tom cat and dead leaves and woodlice and cards from the Rawleigh's man. But there was a definite scarcity of dignified white-haired scholars in well-cut dark suits and horn-rimmed glasses.

So I leaned my bicycle against the side of the house and briefly enjoyed the spectacle. Then he spoke. A beautiful cultured voice in keeping with his air of erudition, and what it said was both relevant and practical.

"Hand me the bread," he murmured melodiously. I did. Then I passed him the eggs and the cheese and the jar of marmite, and balanced a lettuce on top. Such was my confidence in distinguished-looking white-haired strangers.

"Mrs Bream?" he asked. "My name is Newall – principal of . . . "

"Impossible!"

He raised his eyebrows, so I hastened to explain that it was not his fitness for the position which I questioned, but the fact that an application posted by me at eight o'clock in the morning could produce a personal visit by him at three-thirty in the afternoon. For the last few weeks I had been looking regularly through the "Situations Vacant" column and that morning I had posted seven applications. One was for "fast accurate typist", which I wasn't; one for "usherette must have neat appearance", which I hadn't; two were for part-time clerical work, one for "sandwich making mornings only", another for "capable woman take charge", and one, just to round things off and because I had a stamp left, was in reply to an advertisement for teaching staff in a secondary school. Being unaware of the desperate teacher shortage, I had not expected a response to this one at all, and it was a shock to see a headmaster appear so promptly. Moreover, he seemed to be eyeing me with the eager gleam of a naturalist who has glimpsed a notornis in the undergrowth. This too was a change. I had already been interviewed for several positions with no greater success than the promise of "We'll let you know", which they seldom did.

"We have a private bag," explained the headmaster, as he deposited my groceries on the kitchen table, "and the letter you posted this morning has already reached us. We are most interested in your application. *Most* interested. You have impressive academic qualifications." He stepped neatly over the Meccano windmill, made a detour round the roller skates, and followed me into the lounge.

"You . . . er . . . have children?"

I cleared away the latest copies of *The Phantom* to allow him to sit down. Then I drew up a chair and regarded him more closely. Yes, he was surely a fine headmaster. He had a quiet but resonant voice, beautifully modulated. It flowed in well-turned balanced phrases which seemed to compose themselves without any conscious effort on his part. Periodic sentences mainly. Ciceronic rhythm. A classical scholar, I decided. One steeped in his learning until it had become a part of him, permeating his voice, his diction, and even his aspect. I wondered whether his calm, unhurried tone persisted when he was quelling small unruly boys. I had known another voice like that once. It had belonged to an Anglican vicar with a fat stomach, who spoke in church like an archangel, and behaved in his own home like a spoiled puppy. But this voice wasn't quite the same – there was something more to it – something forceful underlying the words, something that told of determination and self-possession and power.

" . . . . . if that would be satisfactory?" I came to with a jolt and realised that the voice had paused, and that lost in its music I had ignored its message.

"I think so," I mumbled hastily in confusion, and with those few careless words threw aside for the next decade my comfort, my health, my good eyesight, and my mental composure.

"Then that's settled," said the voice, with a puzzling note of relief. "We shall expect you tomorrow morning."

"I think you will like the staff," he continued. "Our Senior Mistress, Miss Ferguson, is . . . well, about your age, but a very nice person." I vaguely resented the "but" and decided that you should never judge a headmaster by his voice. I also realised that I was being pushed adroitly down a road where I had not really intended to travel. I must get out of this. I must explain while there was still time. But how could I express it? Should I say "You see I didn't really mean to apply – it was just that I thought it was all right to put in an application because no one would take any notice of it anyway and it made me feel I was trying which I wasn't because I never did want to teach anyway?"

3

No, that wouldn't do. Not for a person of "impressive academic qualifications", and not when he had taken the trouble of coming to interview me.

I protested feebly.

"I haven't got a gown."

"You will not need a gown. I wear a gown. Miss Ferguson wears a gown to assembly. The First Assistant wears a gown. But since so many of the technical masters with excellent attainments in their trade have no academic degree, gowns are not worn by the majority of the staff."

"I'm too old, perhaps?"

"We prefer our female assistants to be mature, and to have *had* their families." A slight shade of bitterness passed over his face. "We have had so many young married women – but never for long. And there is also a certain advantage in having brought up children of your own."

"My degree subjects have not been kept up to date."

This time there was definite amusement in his eyes, although it was not until later that I realised why. "I doubt if you will find that a very great handicap." He rose. I was still struggling.

"I have had no experience."

"I feel sure you will manage. We shall expect you tomorrow." He said goodbye and added as final encouragement: "And you're not entirely without experience – remember, you *did* go to Training College."

Yes, I remembered. When he had left I sat down to a large pot of strong China tea and went on remembering. True, I had been to Training College. It had been nearly twenty years ago, and I had not really enjoyed it. There had then been no separate Training College for secondary school teachers, and I had been one of a small group of University graduates among 300 other

4

students. In an establishment designed and geared for primary teaching, we had been an intrusion and a nuisance. One lecturer had greeted us, at his first lesson, with "Good morning, I do NOT LIKE graduates." In case we doubted his word he devoted the year to proving this statement, a project he carried out with marked success. There were two other lecturers who constantly expected us to feel "superior" because we came from the University. Their policy was to provide a remedy before the disease appeared, to treat us with prophylactic injections of sarcasm and abuse, in order to reduce us to a state of humiliation and depression before the mildest symptom of "superiority" should be seen.

"*You*," they would say, "will doubtless find all these notes beneath the level of your great intellects." "Of course you learned graduates know *all* about education." "Kindly bear with my humble exposition of these elementary details." "If you scholars will graciously condescend to add this fact to your vast knowledge."

They were excellent men – fine, upright, earnest teachers, skilled in their particular branch of study. They simply didn't like newly qualified graduates. And why should they? I don't like pickled onions, and I would not presume to question their taste. But it was unfortunate, as they destroyed our enthusiasm, and instilled in most of us a hatred of Training College and a dread of teaching. Not even the help of the other lecturers – the warm kindliness of the woman who took English, for instance, and the infectious energy of the art teacher – and not even the good-natured acceptance of us shown by the 300 non-graduates, with some of whom we made lasting friendships, could soften the rejection we felt that year.

Still, there had been the periods spent out in schools.

5

These had been useful and interesting. Two-thirds of the year was spent in the Training College. There we made little paper bags, we dipped our fingers in tempera paint and drew squiggly patterns on sheets of paper, we tried without any success to play cricket, we read set books on Child Development and the Adolescent Mind, and we attended lectures. But for the rest of the year we were sent out to various schools where we stayed for a few weeks observing, learning, and being given experience in taking lessons. The staff at the schools had always been kind and helpful and we had learned much from them.

But as I had chosen to train for primary school teaching, I had been sent to only one secondary school. It was one of the oldest and best schools in the city – a famous boys' school which was then employing a few women staff members.

Yes, I remembered. As I thought about it and poured myself another cup of tea, my first day as a student there came back clearly.

I was the only student. I reported to the Principal's office. He handed me a timetable, told me never, *never* to say "Righto", and passed me on to a tall graceful woman who carried a globe of the world and wore her clothes like a top fashion model. She frightened me. It was morning interval, so she led me to the staffroom.

It · was, I knew, the staffroom of a celebrated school, a staffroom soaked in tradition, and I stepped respectfully and gingerly in, almost fearing to trip over one of the long-established roots. There were books everywhere – books on shelves, books on tables, books on the window sills, and small piles of books on the floor by the walls. Over all was a strong smell of stale tobacco smoke.

We were the first to arrive.

"Students take their tea with the staff here," said my guide. "At some schools they're not allowed in the staffroom at all. But we're quite democratic here, so make yourself at home. I'll get your tea for you today. Do sit down."

I looked at a long line of chairs in a row under the windows. There was one armchair, faded but inviting. I passed that and chose a simple austere construction with a hard back.

"Not there!" called my guide hastily. I jumped up in alarm.

"That's the First Assistant's," she explained. "We never sit there." I moved on a couple. "And that's the Head of English."

"Where would you like me to sit? Does each teacher have his own?"

She considered. "No one uses that armchair."

I sat in the armchair, which immediately lowered me almost to floor level, as if to emphasise my lowly and barely tolerated presence in that seat of learning.

"Have you a cup? No, I suppose you haven't. You can have Mr Houghton's today – he's away with the 'flu." She handed me my tea and a plate of biscuits. One chocolate finger rested in glorious command on top of the pile. Obviously the First Assistant's. I passed over a couple of orange creams and pulled at a plain sugared oblong with a broken edge. I was doubtful whether students were really permitted to eat biscuits.

"Well, you're all right now," said my guide. She picked up her globe and floated from the room. The staff began coming in, taking their tea and sitting down. I soon had a moustached young man on my left.

"Student?" he asked. I nodded.

"Have I got you?"

"I don't know."

A middle-aged woman sat down on my right. She had a kindly face and she turned to me with a smile.

"Student?"

"Yes."

"Have I got you?"

"I don't know." It didn't seem polite to say "That depends who you are – who are you?"

The man three chairs away leaned forward. "I'm Bowman – science. Have I got you?"

"I don't think so. I don't take science."

"Pity. I could have used some help."

They lost interest in me, and I listened to the conversation, which was exclusively about school. Young Williamson's biology had improved, the prefects had done a good job Friday morning, the new maps had arrived, Schulton of 4A was becoming far too lazy. I heard no mention of anything but school affairs and was rather surprised. No "beer, women, racehorses or politics" which I had been taught were the topics of all men's conversation. These men seemed absorbed in their work and their pupils. I could not understand why the chairs were all placed in a row. It must have been another tradition or perhaps it was designed to restrict the sound of their discussions to a seemly level.

"Jarvis has done it again," said my left-hand neighbour suddenly.

"I told you he would," said a man at the tea counter. "You wouldn't believe me, but I knew he would."

This was a subject of great importance, for private talk stopped at once and all listened intently.

"I'd better see him," said the First Assistant – at least the occupant of the First Assistant's chair.

"I did. Yesterday," remarked a burly grim-faced giant in sports clothes. "A couple of sixes." This sounded rather severe to me. I knew discipline was maintained

8

strictly at the school, but Jarvis's crime must have been a dreadful one to merit such punishment.

"Not enough," said the First Assistant. "Not nearly enough. Bring him to me at lunch time. We'll get to work on him together." He caught sight of me. "Student? Good morning. I haven't got you. But want any help come along." He ambled off.

My matronly neighbour turned to me.

"It's nearly bell-time," she said. "Do you know where to go? Would you like me to show you?"

"Jarvis . . . " I murmured faintly. "Are they really going to . . . ?"

"Yes, he'll probably make the first eleven – their latest discovery, and only a third-former. They've got to try him out some more first. I can't say I'm much interested really – I never did understand cricket. Now where is your timetable?"

But my neatly drawn-up timetable was never used, for at that moment the Headmaster entered the room and sought me out.

"Mr Card's away. He had a slight accident on the way to school. You don't mind taking over his classes for us while he's away, do you? Excellent experience for you, you know, excellent experience. Really the best way to learn. Quite the best. A great opportunity for you. This way."

He led me outside and across the playground to a group of shabby wooden buildings, each looking like the product of a passionate affair between a discarded army hut and a hay barn. "Seen our prefabs? We hope to get a new block soon but we have to use these in the meantime. Mr Card has all his classes in this one. Come in, come in."

Mr Card had broken his ankle and for the whole of my three weeks at that school, I taught in his hut. Well

9

perhaps "taught" is the wrong word. The work was set for each form and sent in daily by Mr Card. It was brought over to me by a prefect. I wrote it on the board, I watched the pupils do it, and then I marked their books. There was no problem of controlling the classes, as the hut was a double unit, and I kept all the boys firmly under the thumb of the man next door. He was very good to me and the boys' classes who came to me in succession were obviously in fear of him or of his cane. The wall was thin, and at the slightest suggestion of talkativeness or even undue shuffling of chairs, he would appear at my door.

The boys tolerated me, with a bored superficial respect, using me as a dictionary and occasionally asking for explanations or help. There was a brief spell of friendliness in the second week, when one of them – I don't know how – discovered that I owned a motor bike. For two days they thought I was human after all, and even grinned me a welcome when they arrived. But when I couldn't, on request, name the birth year of my Ariel or the exact cubic capacity of its engine, they wrote me off again, as just another woman.

I did not go over to the staffroom for morning tea or lunch, as I felt out of place in such an atmosphere. Instead I used to walk around the grounds, watching the sports practices, or the groups of writhing, struggling, wrestling arms and legs on the grass as half a dozen boys would each try to choke the breath out of his friends. I spoke to no teachers other than my neighbour, no one came to watch my teaching or enquire after my welfare, and at the end of my three weeks I quietly left. I made one final trip over to the main school, to say goodbye to the headmaster and tell him my time was up. He said oh dear, oh dear, he would have to make some other arrangements for the next week, he thanked me for my help and felt sure that the period there would have been most valuable to me, most valuable indeed, really excellent experience. He added that he had been in touch with the Training College authorities, explained the situation and asked them not to come to inspect my teaching as in the circumstances it would cause too much disruption to the school. As I was not destined for secondary teaching, they had agreed.

I had found those three weeks utterly exhausting, and was glad to leave. Although there had been no discipline problems, thanks to my friendly neighbour, the strain of coping with the questions of intelligent pupils and the problems of duller ones, the marking of exercises at night, the presentation of the small amount of new work which I had to introduce, the constant attention necessary all day, and the mental strain, had all left me with a fixed resolve that teaching was not for me.

And that had been twenty years ago.

Chapter 2

It was a two-storey brick building, neither handsome nor inviting. It grew wearily out of the pavement, with a bored, matter-of-fact air, its doors opening directly onto the street – no trees, or flowers or drive or any of that nonsense. Almost opposite the main entrance were the city gas works, at one side the railway station, and I found out later that the school made a full-time hobby of absorbing the soot from one and the smell from the other. I also learned that it had been built at the beginning of the century and had quite an honourable history. But it had not mellowed with age. The mortar was crumbling and the brickwork discoloured, yet it had none of the venerable benevolence of the old University buildings, or the Girls' High School. It wasn't exactly like a prison, it wasn't quite a "satanic mill". It was simply a tired, business-like stack of old bricks with a job to do.

I pushed open the double doors and walked in. Not so bad inside. A wide stairway faced me, to left and right of it ran corridors, laid with brightly polished blue lino. The walls were painted light blue, mushroom and white, and along them were hung enormous framed photographs. A man with a beard, a man without a beard,

13

a row of men in gowns, another man with another beard
– they seemed to stretch right down the corridors,
broken only by an occasional red box labelled "Fire
alarm. DO NOT TOUCH." It was not as dismal as
the outside appearance of the school, but I noticed that
none of those faces on the wall was particularly cheerful
or cheering. Ex-principals, perhaps? Members of boards
of governors? Distinguished old boys? Teachers who had
survived a qualifying period? Or teachers who had not
survived? I wished one of them would smile at me.

There was an office to my right, and next to it a door
marked "Principal", against which was leaning, with
an air of unconcern, a tall pale-faced boy. His grey
socks were round his ankles, and his grey shirt had a
button missing, where the thread still showed. His
black hair was uncombed and hung over his forehead.
At my approach he slowly shifted his weight, rolled
over, and leaned against the wall instead of the door.
He didn't look at me – he didn't appear to be looking
at anything. He seemed to be in a semi-comatose state
of dull resignation – whether by nature or through
anticipation of what awaited him beyond the door, I
couldn't decide. I said good morning to him as I
knocked, but he neither looked at me nor replied. There
were no other children in sight.

Although it was quite early, Mr Newall was already at
school. He received me graciously, and as I sat in his
office he told me a little about the school hours and
routine. I would teach English, social studies, typing
and core mathematics, he explained, and the fact that
I knew very little about the last three of these was of
small importance. As two months of the school year
had already elapsed, I would merely have to carry on
with the scheme planned by my predecessors – it sounded
simple enough. From time to time, as he talked to me

there was a brief knock, and a head would show itself round the edge of the door, to give some information or to make an enquiry. The first was that of Miss McComish, who Mr Newall told me was in charge of the girls' homecraft department. Hers was a grey-haired, middle-aged head, with a square capable-looking face on it, and a firm manly voice, which greeted me in hearty tones. I was introduced to each as it appeared, and was beginning to wonder whether it was a time-honoured custom to enter the Principal's office head first – a sign of respect perhaps? – when Miss Ferguson, the Senior Mistress, came in. Not head first, either. She arrived all of one piece, with grace and dignity. She was tall and good-looking; her dress was faultless, her hair smartly, if rather severely, in place, and her eyes were of a glorious deep vandyke brown. She may have been about my age, but she made me feel like a down-at-heel scrub. I went out with her, but I missed her speech of welcome, as I was wondering whether my seams were straight and if I should have worn a hat.

Miss Ferguson led me to the staffroom on the first floor, a large room with windows all along one side overlooking the playground, and on the other, cupboards and bookshelves. The chairs were not in a row here, but placed around two enormous tables, which the teachers used for their morning tea, their lunch, their discussions and their marking. I was shown the cupboard allotted to me, and found that all the textbooks which I would need had already been placed in it by some thoughtful member of the staff. Miss Ferguson introduced several of the men to me. There were some whose disembodied heads I had already met, and the others all knew my name. "That's because you're an Event," one explained. "We knew you were about to happen. We've been working one short on the staff for three weeks, so the news of your appointment soon flew round us all last night. We shan't have to take two classes in the same room any more – and we might even get some marking periods back. So you see how welcome you are. I just hope you stay for a while."

Other remarks were friendly but disturbing.

"You look healthy," said one man. "I give you two weeks."

"Passing through?" asked another.

The women teachers – about seven in all – were in a group at one end of the room. We joined them. I was introduced and all smiled encouragingly at me. Too encouragingly. It alarmed me. They didn't do that in offices or factories when they met new staff. This was a "Be brave – take heart – this may hurt a little" smile, and I made a mental note to practise it for use on the next newcomer.

"Come over to assembly with Mrs Rose and me," said Miss Burton, a pretty young dark girl. "We're new this year too, and we know what it's like when you go up on the stage for the first time, and those nine hundred and fifty pairs of eyes look you over." Mrs Rose agreed. She was a pleasant but tired looking woman in her twenties.

We walked down the back stairs, and across the playground to the school hall, where assembly was held each morning. I could see that the school property occupied a whole city block, and the buildings on it left very little playing area. I had been wrong about the trees, though. There was one – one solitary cherished oak tree, in the middle of the playground, which I was told had been there since the foundation of the school. The ground was paved all around it, as space was so precious, but wise successive governors had refused to sacrifice it entirely. It was known and referred to simply

16

as "The Tree".

Assembly followed the traditional pattern. After a hymn and the Lord's Prayer, the school sat down, and then, from my position on the stage where the women staff occupied the front row of seats, I was able to examine the pupils in the body of the hall. The boys wore grey shirts and shorts; the girls had a navy-blue gymdress over a white blouse, and some wore navy blazers. I looked more closely at the girls in the front rows just below me. Navy-blue is a depressing colour, and one which is difficult to keep clean. Some of the girls had made the most of it, and had a neat, fresh appearance. Others wore grubby blouses and spotted gymdresses; they had laddered stockings and tousled hair. Hair of all colours. Unnaturally bright yellow, tomato red, jet black. Some was twisted into strange shapes, some hung lankly – there were pigtails, curls, bobs, cottage loaves, plaits and haystacks. I could see, even from the stage, that one girl in the second row wore bright blue eyeshadow. They were all of course examining me with an equally close scrutiny, and doubtless summing up my potential as a future adversary.

Mr Newall spoke briefly to the school on a variety of subjects, from chewing gum to basketball, then left the stage, and the staff filed out after him.

"What do you think of them?" asked Miss Burton, as we strolled back to the staffroom.

"The children? They look harmless enough."

"Don't be deceived," said Mrs Rose. "That innocent veneer covers a hard core of stubborn unmanageability, doesn't it, Mrs Donning?"

A plump little woman with merry eyes had come to meet us. "I missed assembly," she said, "to clean up that terrible mess in the art room. Do you know what Heather McNeil did yesterday, Mrs Bream?"

17

I never discovered what Heather had done, for at that moment a tall, thin, bespectacled man approached us and beckoned me aside.

"I'm good," he announced.

As he had obviously sought me out to say this, I did not fall into the blunder I might have made. I replied "good morning" instead.

"Good," he repeated, "L.C. Good. First Assistant. Pleased you could join us. How are you?"

"Goo – fine, thank you."

"Here's a list of the forms you will teach today. Come with me and I'll show you your room. I can't give you your permanent timetable yet, because we want you to take Mr Pellowe's classes for a few days while he's away."

"Sick?"

"He received a paper pellet in the eye. I assure you, Mrs Bream, that it is *not* very amusing to be hit in the eye with a paper pellet." I quite believed him, and translated his remark into "Wipe that silly grin off your face, woman." I did. I didn't think it was amusing either, and my smile had been one of nervous apprehension, not enjoyment. But he had not quite forgiven me.

"Mr Pellowe has had a very bad eye," he continued grimly. "He had to go to a specialist with it. And *you* are now about to take that same class. However, I've allotted you the room opposite my office, which will be a great help to you. I always try to give that room to newcomers who have had no experience in teaching. You have your own room here, you understand, and the children come to you each period. I have Mr Pellowe's first class already lined up for you outside your door. It's 4B2 – not a bad form really, in spite of that pellet. Mr Pellowe takes them for English and they will have something to go on with."

He was leading me downstairs as he spoke, and we

18

turned into one of the corridors. About forty girls and boys were lined up in a double row outside the room at the far end. At the approach of the First Assistant they straightened and became quiet. He introduced me briefly and then turned into his study opposite. The pupils looked at me with interest and I at them. Most of them were bigger than I, half at least were boys. They waited. I waited. I realised that I had no idea of the simplest routines of school procedure. Here I had my pupils in front of me, but what next? Did I tell them to enter the room? Did I go first and hope they would follow? In my own school days the teachers had come to us as we waited in our own form room. We used to stand up as we heard each teacher's footsteps approaching, and those in the front desks vied with one another for the privilege of holding open the door. I didn't think there would be any ardent competition among these pupils to hold the classroom door open for me. So I opened it quickly myself and the question of procedure and precedence was quickly solved. The column changed at once into a heaving irregular mass of bodies, books and satchels, trying to force itself all of a piece through a totally inadequate aperture. I flattened myself against the door jamb to avoid permanent injury. When all were in I followed. Then I shut the door. The First Assistant had left his wide open, doubtless with a view to helping me, but I did not want my first attempts at teaching to be visible or audible to any experienced teacher, least of all the First Assistant. I wished there had not been a glass panel set into the top portion of the door – or that I could at least have had a thick dark blind to pull down over it.

The pupils were now sitting at their desks, and surprisingly quiet as they regarded me. There was no platform in the room but underneath the blackboard was

19

a low, narrow seating bench. I climbed on this as being a better vantage ground. It wobbled, and so did I. This was rather disconcerting just now, but proved to be quite an asset during the year – I learned in subsequent months to ride my bench, and I could give effective thumps with the short leg to emphasise my statements, to add weight to a threat, or to signal that I wanted the attention of the whole class. But during my first encounter with a massed squad of opposing teenagers its rocking movements added to my total feeling of insecurity.

I looked at the class. When would the pellets begin?

"Are you going to take us?" asked a girl in the front row.

"Just while Mr Pellowe's away. Open your books."

"I haven't got mine."

"Neither have I."

"Neither have I."

More than half the class were without their English books.

"But you knew it was English, didn't you? Why didn't you bring your books?"

"Mr Pellowe's away. We didn't know we'd have English."

In my innocence I believed this. I had a lot to learn. A hand was up.

"Where did you come from, Mrs Bream? Are you going to stay here?"

"I shall be here this year."

"Do you like teaching?"

Here was a good opportunity to learn something about the school.

"I don't know yet. Suppose you tell me a little about this College."

"It's a rotten dump."

"You mustn't say that. It's a fine school." A roar of

20

hearty laughter greeted this, and I weakly changed the subject.

"Since you haven't brought your books, we had better do some revision this period. What English have you done this year? You, by the window?"

He by the window promptly looked out of the aforesaid window and pretended not to have heard. But his neighbour answered with a shrug: "Not much, I guess." There was a pause.

"Pronouns," said a girl at the back suddenly.

"Very well, what is a pronoun?"

She didn't know. Silence.

"Can anyone tell me what a pronoun is?" Silence. "Can anyone give me an example of a pronoun?" No one could. No one, obviously, cared. A boy in front said they had never been told nothink about them. A girl across the aisle said they had so. The class said they had so. The boy said well *he* hadn't. The point was debated hotly and I looked quickly round the room to see if anyone was rolling a paper pellet. ("Well of course they weren't," said my son scornfully that evening. "You don't roll them in class. You make them beforehand and keep your pockets full." So that's what had blocked the washing machine! Yes, I had a lot to learn.)

I was not too enthusiastic about pronouns myself, and was sorry that they had somehow been dragged in to foul up my first lesson. But since they had intruded, I explained as best I could their character, their means of identification, and their *raison d'être*. No one showed the least interest. But there were no pellets yet, and the class was fairly quiet. Bored, I guessed, and waiting to be entertained. I understood that I was being given a chance. I wondered whether the First Assistant was listening outside the door.

"Which books have you read? I hope you all read a lot.

21

It helps your English. You" – I pointed at random to a plump red-head – "what have you read lately?"

"*A Tale of Two Cities.*"

Bless her heart! I must have misjudged them all.

"That's fine. Who wrote it?"

"It's a classic."

"Yes, I suppose it is. Who was the author?"

"It's a classic."

"But who *wrote* it?"

She looked puzzled, and so did her neighbours.

"It's a Classic. Look, I've got it. See?" She pulled a ragged paper bundle from her satchel and handed it to me. It was a Classic. A Classic Comic, condensing into thirty odd pages of boxed off little coloured pictures, the hundred and seventy thousand words of the famous novel. I pointed out on it the author's name, and the brief biography on the back page. I spoke of his other works, and I even turned to hunt for chalk and write some titles on the blackboard, which I thought was a rather brave thing to do. But then they hadn't shot Mr Pellowe in the back.

"What else have you read?"

"*King Solomon's Mines.*"

"A Classic?"

They laughed at my ignorance. "It's a book. They gave us one each. We read it in class."

"Tell me about it."

The lesson dragged slowly on. But there were no pellets – at least I felt none. When the bell rang I was still whole.

I was better prepared with a plan of action when the next class cascaded in. They were fifth form boys.

"You all have something to get on with," I announced hopefully. "Get on with it." They looked doubtful, but one by one drew out a book or a pad from their bags.

It was an uneventful lesson – a fairly calm forty minutes. I suspected noughts and crosses in the back row, but was too cowardly to investigate. There was a continuous low hum of voices, but all appeared busy. I dared not take my eyes off the class, and at intervals said "Silence!" in what I hoped was a voice of firm authority. As no one took any notice, I suppose it wasn't. But there was no major incident, and thank goodness, no pellets. When the bell rang for interval I was quick off the mark and reached the corridor first, leaving behind me a sound of shrieks, blows, banging desk tops, overturned chairs and unidentifiable thuds. I made thankfully for the staffroom and a cup of tea. Well, my morning had not been entirely wasted. I had at least taught one class who wrote *A Tale of Two Cities*. (I hadn't, of course. When I had occasion to take them one day several weeks later, they swore they had never heard of the fellow.)

"Good news," said the First Assistant, as he politely handed me the milk. "Mr Pellowe will be back at school tomorrow, so we can revert to normal timetable. And I have managed to free you for all the rest of today. Would you care to observe?"

"Observe?"

"Yes, I'm sure none of the staff would mind. Just go along to their rooms, tell them why you've come, and sit at the back while they teach. You will get quite a few tips that way, since you're unfamiliar with teaching techniques."

So he *had* been listening at the door! But it seemed an excellent idea, and for the rest of that day, I observed. I did not detect any cordial welcome on the part of most teachers into whose rooms I walked, and had I been more versed in the trials of teaching I would never have considered adding my presence to all their other difficulties. At the time I foolishly thought they would be

23

pleased and flattered.

I wandered around the school, from room to room and building to building, choosing my observees simply by the presence or otherwise of an empty desk in their rooms, as seen through the glass portion of the door.

My first visit was to Mr Bowron, who took senior mathematics in the room next to mine. He was sitting at his table, surrounded by pupils with books in hand. The rest of the class were talking among themselves, but spared me a passing interest.

"It's the new one," I heard one girl say clearly. Her group gazed at me speculatively. Mr Bowron was startled by my request. He wore an unhappy distraught expression.

"But I'm not teaching," he protested. "I'm marking, and there's nothing to watch in that. You'd better go to Room Five – Mr Rowlings. LEAVE THAT ALONE!" I gathered the last remark was not addressed to me, and quietly left.

"Bream or Cream or something," I heard as I went out.

Mr Rowlings's room was a few doors down the corridor. He had a large class of boys, but there was one empty desk. He was a tall man with a wide flat face, black hair which stood straight up, and enormous shoulders. A cane lay conspicuously across his table. The room was very quiet. Mr Rowlings motioned to his boys to stand up as I entered, and he came over to meet me. He shook my hand, welcomed me to the school and showed me courteously to the empty desk. The boys were still standing, motionless and silent, so silent in fact that my request was heard by all, and rumour later spread not only among the pupils but among their parents also, that I represented the Child Welfare Department, and was teaching for a few weeks at the school while I investigated, and reported on, Mr Rowlings's somewhat

24

severe disciplinary measures. I learned that his caning stroke was so powerful that he broke the skin with every cut, and had been directed by the Headmaster that he must cane with the left hand only. This, the boys told me, was far worse than before, because although his left arm was almost as strong as his right, and he still drew blood, his aim was not nearly so accurate, and a cut across the back of the knees or just above the tailbone could put one off cricket for a week. They did not resent this – after all, they pointed out, he *was* right-handed and couldn't be expected to get a bull's eye each time when so unfairly handicapped. They blamed the Headmaster for their wounds, not Mr Rowlings, whom they liked very much, and who was extraordinarily good to them in many ways. The only solution was to behave well in his class, which they did, making up in all the others for fun lost in his. This caused a mild resentment on the part of teachers less well physically equipped.

"They come to me straight after Rowlings on Monday," complained Mr Frieze, the music master. "After a whole forty minutes of being quiet, you can just imagine how they relax. Music's bad enough to take at any time – when I'm at the piano I can't see what they're up to – but taking music after Rowlings . . . ! It's hell, pure hell!"

"And what about me?" said Mr Watts, a young history teacher. "I have them three times a week just *before* he does, so they use my period to limber up and exercise in readiness for sitting still in his room. And they tell one another all the news they want to impart before interval, because they know they won't have another chance till his lesson is over."

Apart from the unnatural silence, there was little to observe in Mr Rowlings's room. The boys read in turn

25

from a textbook, with no comment from the teacher. Then they were set an exercise. I wandered round the room, looking at their books, which were untidy and unmarked. "He never marks," explained Miss Burton later. "He doesn't need to. But he does lots of other things for them."

The next room proved to be that of Mrs Rose, whom I knew to be a recent arrival at the school, so I did not stay. Her class were talking, but they were also working. She gave me a friendly "Hi!" with her back turned to them, and invited me to have lunch the next day at her home.

I passed on to Miss Harris, who was teaching social studies to a mixed fourth form. She was a tall blonde girl and would have been very pretty without the frown of worry which she now wore. The room was buzzing with voices, and above it she was trying to give directions. "Oh please don't come here," she pleaded. "It's bad enough without anyone." I agreed, and left.

Miss Ferguson's own class was quiet and seemed to be attentive, but she too asked me not to remain. "I have nothing new prepared," she explained. "Another day perhaps?"

I was taking this opportunity to explore the school. I discovered the library underneath the Assembly Hall, I watched the sports mistress, Miss White, taking physical education in the playground, and then I walked over to the Technical buildings – the carpentry and engineering workshops. There was quite a different atmosphere here. All the boys were happily engrossed in their practical work. I was willingly shown round by the teachers, and the boys demonstrated several machines for me. But the explanations were lost on me as my ears were not as accustomed as theirs to the hum of machinery, and I heard very little of what was said. Nor did I share the masculine love of whirring wheels, rapidly moving belts and sharp lethal blades. I was secretly glad to leave.

I walked round the playground, examined several sheds, prefabricated buildings, and storerooms, then made my way back to the main school, and continued my "observation" in the classrooms. The reception of the teachers varied from "Oh, for heaven's sake, NO!" or "*Please* go away!" to a shrug and a "Well if you really want to – I don't know what good it's going to do you." One man stared in astonishment and said "What the heck for?"

Miss Burton's class all rose to their feet as soon as I entered. "It was your white hair," Miss Burton explained to me later. "As soon as you had left one little girl said 'Mrs Bream's important, isn't she? She must be very high up.' I told her yes, you were." I was grateful for this attempt to invest me with some authority in advance. My hair proved to be an advantage in the days to come, too. It was the first time in my life that I was to reap any benefit from the family curse of premature greying.

Upstairs were the clothing and cooking rooms. The clothing pupils were busy trying to pattern together little coloured strands of cotton, to illustrate the various weaves of materials. Their books were delightful, with samples and illustrations of threads, notes on dressmaking, and pasted cuttings. Clothing was either a well-liked subject or a well-controlled department. Miss Tulley, a tall thin middle-aged woman, told me she had been there six years – almost a record at the school.

The cooking department was busy too. The room was noisy, Miss McComish not seeming to mind a constant chatter from the girls as they opened ovens, washed tools, and moved about the model benches. I walked behind one oven and found a little girl crouched on the

27

floor with *True Romances* clutched in her hands. She was too absorbed to notice me, and I decided it was not my place to interfere. The oven sheltered her on one side, the wall on another and a cooking bench behind, so she had a fairly good chance of finishing her story. The food smelled delicious.

"It's a good roast dinner," said Miss McComish, "and they'll eat it before they go home. I know it's not exactly the hour of the day for a roast dinner, but have you seen what they bring for lunch? I doubt if some of them have had a square meal for weeks, poor kids."

"Do they pay for the ingredients?"

"They pay half-a-crown a term, which barely covers the salt they throw over each other when my back is turned. But we manage. I cut down on other things out of the homecraft grant. And someone gave us a case of carrots the other day." She bustled away, and I strongly suspected that much of the material used was provided by Miss McComish herself.

I visited several other rooms, and noticed that in nearly all the practical classes, except art, where it was difficult to sort out Mrs Donning from the swarming chattering mass, the pupils were happily occupied and moderately well behaved. But in academic classes there was noticeable resistance to learning and to authority. At the end of that day I was left with the impression of a teaching staff struggling vainly but valiantly against an inexorably advancing tide of noise and movement. It was like a forced obstacle race, which all teachers had been employed to undergo. Some tried strenuously to make themselves heard, some shouted and obtained momentary silence, some, like Mrs Donning, had apparently resigned themselves to teaching against a background accompaniment of voices, whose volume varied from room to room. There were children standing in the corridor outside nearly every door in the main building – the worst offenders had been turned out of the room in an attempt better to control the remainder.

I did not learn how to teach from my observation visits. Nor did I gain any pointers on subduing a class sufficiently to enable me to teach them. But I did gain something. I discovered that the teachers' work was on the whole well prepared and carefully presented, that much trouble had been taken to give new material in a form which could be understood and assimilated, and which would arouse interest where interest was possible. I saw that most of the pupils' work had been meticulously marked, that the comments written on it were encouraging and helpful, that a determined effort was being made to force knowledge into unwilling heads, that a genuine desire to help – both in and out of the classroom – was a part of every teacher in the school.

I also gained a thumping headache and a fit of panic. The lack of discipline astonished me, and I looked forward with dread to my own coming struggles. If experienced teachers failed to control these children, what could I do? But my respect for my new profession and its members had risen considerably.

Chapter 3

"It is most unwise," said the First Assistant reprovingly
next morning, "to leave your room before your class does.
I noticed you did so yesterday – in fact I had to go in
myself to bring those people to order and see that they
walked out quietly. They must not be left alone in the
rooms – we've had too many windows and chairs broken.
And a nose as well last week."

"A teacher's?" The profession must be even more
dangerous than I had thought.

"No, Mrs Bream. Had a teacher been present and
doing his duty, the accident would not have occurred
at all. Always see that you are the last to leave a room.
Make a special point of it."

We were walking up the stairs together before school.

"Very well," I said, "I'll remember that. But I doubt
if it will make much difference whether I'm there or not."

"You must see that it *does* make a difference. You
appeared to be managing quite well yesterday," he
added encouragingly. "I didn't hear much noise from
your room during those first two periods. Did you find
your observation helpful? Yes, I thought you would."

"I feel helpless and quite incompetent."

"There's no need. Today you will meet your own

31

classes for the first time, so make it clear to them right from the beginning that you will stand no nonsense."

"How?"

"Show them your authority."

"How?"

"Just be firm. Demand obedience and see that you get it. Don't speak until the room is silent, and then speak quietly. *Never* raise your voice. Silence is far more effective, and a quiet command will bring results where a shout will not. Now when your class is inclined to be talkative, you will find that . . . " He stopped suddenly, as a small boy came out of the classroom we had just reached at the head of the stairs. "YOU!" roared the First Assistant. "WHAT ARE YOU DOING INSIDE? DON'T YOU KNOW YOU ARE NOT SUPPOSED TO BE UP HERE BEFORE SCHOOL? IF I EVER CATCH YOU AGAIN . . . " His voice boomed down the corridors. The boy murmured a "Yessir" and hastily disappeared down the back stairs.

"What were we saying, Mrs Bream? Ah yes, don't worry if at first you can't maintain an absolutely quiet class. Control is something which comes with experience. Refer to me anyone who gives you trouble."

We entered the staffroom.

"What, you back again?" said Miss Harris cheerfully. "Congratulations and good morning."

"Of course I'm back. Wonderful job this – and I've heard a rumour that we even get paid as well."

"Look at her," said Mrs Donning, the art teacher. "Still in the bloom of her youth. Still smiling. Hope and confidence clouding her vision. Wait until tomorrow. Wait until next week. Watch the wrinkles grow and the smile fade and the shoulders sag – watch the snarl develop, watch her eyes narrow and her forehead furrow and her pleasant nature change into a warped and bitter hatred of all mankind. Wait for the nervous tics to develop – the twitching cheek muscles, the pulse below the ear, the spasmodic jerking of one arm . . . "

"The indigestion, the ulcers, the backache . . . " continued Mrs Rose.

"The pains in her head, the eyestrain," contributed Miss Burton.

"The insomnia, the rheumatism . . . "

"Nonsense!" interrupted Miss McComish. "No one ever got rheumatism from teaching. So don't you worry any more about rheumatism, Mrs Bream. We had a teacher last year who stayed just one day, then she'd had enough. She rang up next morning to say she had taken a job selling cakes in a shop and not to bother about her umbrella, thank you. We could keep it as a defence weapon for the classroom."

"Mrs Bream is made of stronger metal," said Miss Harris.

"That type fall the hardest," said Miss Tulley, the clothing teacher. "Remember Miss Nowles last year? And Mrs Sweeney?"

"What happened to them?" asked Mrs Rose. "I wasn't here last year."

"Nervous breakdowns. Mrs Sweeney was one of our firmest disciplinarians. You never heard a sound from her classes and she always looked placid and contented and very very capable. She never complained either. We used to envy her. Then one morning interval she walked into the staffroom, gave a sort of strangled sob and collapsed in a heap on the floor. We took her home in a taxi and she was in hospital for three weeks. Just nervous exhaustion. But don't let us frighten you, Mrs Bream. She recovered – well, almost – and took a light clerical job in the Forestry."

"You're not frightening me. What about Miss

33

Nowles?"

"Just a slow disintegration in her case. We watched it day by day. Interesting. Like an Aspro in a glass of water. She got very dreamy after a while and had a lost look all the time. She couldn't remember things and turned up in odd places at the wrong times. She left, of course."

"Yes, a week after I arrived," said Mrs Donning. "I remember how she took all the fifth form biology pupils over to the bicycle shed one day, and Mr Good brought them back. You can't escape the corrosive effects of this job, Mrs Bream – it's just a matter of how long they take to develop in each of us and what particular shape they come in."

"If what you say is true, Mrs Donning, why have you no signs of collapse or neurosis? You take all the girls, so you must have the worst pupils among them. Yet I see no wrinkles or careworn expression on your face."

"I ignore them all," said Mrs Donning. "They can climb on the desks or out the windows or up the walls if they want to. I just shut my ears and eyes to them and get on with my work. But that can't go on for ever. I guess I'll blow up one day."

With this encouragement still ringing in my ears, I walked downstairs after assembly to my first class of the day. This was H3C, who were to be my own form. Each class is allotted a form teacher, who is held responsible throughout the year for their permanent register, their welfare and their general behaviour. It is a convenient arrangement. The threat "I shall tell your form teacher about this" is quite useful ammunition against the third-formers until they learn that their form teacher is as powerless to deal with them as any other. And "a boy of *your* form" is a satisfying way of referring to a malefactor – it implies that misbehaviour in the presence of one teacher might very well be the responsibility of another.

I had been told that my form, H3C, was the lowest stream of the homecraft girls. Thirty-seven of them, but – thank goodness – no boys.

I brought them into my room and when all were seated the class and I looked at each other with interest. There were five Maoris among them and a variety of hair colours and complexions among the others. They did not look unfriendly. Nor did they seem to be greatly subdued by respect for my white hair. I mustn't rely on that too much. I remembered what the First Assistant had advised – be firm right from the start. Well, I was prepared to be. I was prepared for the worst. At this stage my confidence in juvenile human nature was precisely nil. I knew that a teenager was an unhappy blend of depravity and malice, a savage animal against which the only effective weapon was a cane I hadn't got.

"Are you going to be our form teacher?" asked a little plump girl in the front row.

"You know quite well that I am," I said coldly. "The First Assistant has just introduced me and told you so."

The girl smiled at me. "I'm Denise," she said.

"How long are you going to stay?" asked her neighbour, a thin, peroxide blonde.

"She's Lynn," said Denise, jerking a thumb in her direction.

"Where did you come from, Mrs Bream?" asked another girl.

"Do you like this school?"

"Do you like teaching?"

"Do you think it's fair that girls aren't allowed to wear nail polish?"

"You are so, if it's clear, Miss Ferguson said."

"She said natural and mine's natural and I can show her the label if she likes but she still made me take it off.

35

Just because it was pink. Pink's natural. Do you think it's fair, Mrs Bream?"

"Hush. Quiet, everyone!" I replied. Surprisingly they were.

The first thing of course was to get their names. They knew mine. I had been given a roll, but this was no help in identifying the owners of the names on it. I made a rough chart of the room and asked them in turn for their names. I was prepared for trouble here, too, and knew I must be careful. I intended to be one jump in front of them – that would show them that they couldn't fool me. Yes, I knew all about taking names. My young son, a third-former at another school, had briefed me on its dangers, and had carefully outlined for my protection the procedure his own form adopted when left in sole charge of a visiting student. Students, of course, were regarded by the pupils at his school as delightful recreational equipment – a glorious gift from the educational authorities to enliven an otherwise dull weekly routine, and a challenge for the worst of any class's skill in the art of misbehaviour. My son's class counted their students as so many blessings, and enjoyed them to the full. But students were not armed with a cane, and a stage would eventually arrive when the poor victim would seek retaliation which he was unable to deal out himself. He would stride up to my son, for instance.

"*You!*" he would shout. "What's your name?"

My son would hesitate, attempt to look embarrassed and frightened, and after a pause blurt out "Er . . . Bream, sir," as though by sudden inspiration. There would be an immediate protest from the rest of the class.

"Aw, cut it out, Hindmarsh." "You liar, Hindmarsh." "Tell him your name, Hindmarsh." The boy nearest the student would whisper quietly and confidentially

36

"It's Hindmarsh, sir. B. Hindmarsh."

"All right, Hindmarsh," the angry student would say. "Five hundred lines for misbehaviour, and another five hundred for telling lies. I shall report you to your form master."

B. Hindmarsh was duly reported for misconduct, and the form master could only assume that these students did mix classes up so. Of course it wasn't one of *his* boys. Come to think of it, he couldn't remember a Hindmarsh in any of the third forms. Really, these students . . . So the matter was shelved, and B. Hindmarsh remained unpunished, to fight again under the name of R.T. Birdworthy, or Angus McTavish.

I was forewarned and I didn't intend to be caught. Show them from the start that I would stand no nonsense.

The first two names seemed all right. The third girl – a Maori – said "Honeyanne."

Here it was. "None of that!" I snapped. "Give me your correct name at once!"

The class looked indignant. "It *is* her name. She can't help it. We call her Bugs, don't we, Bugs?"

By this time I had found it on the register. Two words. Honey Anne. The surname was Ngatai. I could hardly apologise without seeming to ridicule her name.

"Give it to me again, please," I said. "More slowly."

"Bugs," said the Maori, "Bugs Ngatai."

Honey Anne's name was a difficulty to me for the rest of her stay. I could scarcely address her as Honey. Bugs proved to be rather more fitting – distressingly so at times – but it seemed a little unkind. Anne she would not answer to. So I alternated between "you" and something like "Hunyan" until she left school at the end of the first term.

The name-taking continued. One little girl didn't answer me at all. She just opened her eyes a little wider.

She had a round face and two dark pigtails, the ends of which she held tightly, one in each hand.

"That's Felicity," said Denise. "She's not very bright." She smiled at Felicity, and Felicity smiled at us all.

There was no deception over the names. I completed my chart and ordered the girls to sit in the same seats each day until I had learned which name belonged to whom. They expected me to have done this by the following morning, and looked quite hurt when I had to refer to my chart.

"I'm *Helen*," one would say. "You remember me?"

"Oh yes, of course, Helen," I would reply. I made a smaller chart and kept it in the textbook, where I could consult it unseen. This worked quite well until they changed places against my orders, but with what they considered an incontrovertible reason.

"But I *had* to sit by Sally. I haven't got a book."

"But Heather and Jane aren't speaking, so they *couldn't* sit together. They had a row last night over David Robertson."

"But Jenny asked me to because Susan's away."

This first day, however, I was not expected to know names, and Denise of the front row made a point of telling me at frequent intervals during the lesson who she was. "I'm Denise, remember? And she's Lynn."

I began the lesson. "I shall be taking you for English, as you know. So take out your English textbooks. Well, where *are* they? Weren't you issued with any?" There were five textbooks in the room.

"We thought you might do something else." "We didn't know we were having English." "I've lost mine." "Mine's in my locker." "I lent mine to someone." "Can we do geography this period?" "Can we have a debate?" "Mr Bunting used to tell us about India." "Have you been to India?"

"Well, I must see what your English is like. Take a pen and paper and write me a paragraph on one of these subjects." There was a general shuffle as those with paper willingly distributed it among those who had not. There was another re-distribution of their combined stock of pens, as I wrote some simple topics on the board.

"Can I help Felicity?" someone asked.

"No. Felicity must do her own work."

"She can't do much," said Denise. "She's not very clever."

"Felicity will do her best for me, I'm sure." Felicity smiled.

What was left of the period passed quietly. I walked round the room. Denise had written her name in large capitals across the top of her page, and underlined it. Felicity used big printed letters, and worked slowly, but the content of her paragraph seemed of a standard not much lower than some of the others.

The bell rang, and I took in their papers.

"We stay here, don't we?" they asked.

"Yes," I said. "We do social studies this period. Take out your social study books."

They gasped at this monstrous suggestion. "We have a rest first."

I was uncertain about this. "Do you?" I asked feebly.

They did. It consisted of rearranging their chairs, arguing over someone's visit to the Blue Mill, whatever that was, and (until I objected) doing one another's hair. I gave them four minutes, then told them again to take out their social study books.

Social studies was an innovation since my own school days, and I found it to be a revolting alloy of the worst features of geography and history, two subjects which I had always feared and abhorred. I was not a specialist in either. Geography I had been allowed to abandon at the end of my second high school year, to the great relief of the teaching staff as well as myself, and I had never since felt an overwhelming urge to broaden my knowledge of the subject. I knew the rough position of the four main centres of New Zealand, and the accepted pronunciation of Paraparaumu, and I found this quite adequate for my needs. As for history, I had been forced to bear with that right through school, but I had beaten it. Even when I succumbed resentfully to fate and made an earnest effort to absorb the repulsive stuff – when I stayed up late at night for weeks before the Scholarship exam with Southgate's *Modern English History Book Two* as my companion – when I pasted Causes of the French Revolution on the bathroom mirror – when I ate my breakfast with Brief Notes on Bismarck propped up against the milk jug – even then, with such overwhelming odds against me, I managed to emerge unscathed by any but the most superficial scratches of historical knowledge. It was a remarkable feat.

Well, to learn it had proved impossible, but to teach it might be easier.

To my surprise nearly all of H3C had their social studies books with them. "It's beaut fun," explained Colleen, a bulky six-footer with long straight brown hair. "We like it."

I looked at her exercise book. It was open at a pretty picture of two bright blue rivers, and placed neatly between them was a green moon labelled "Furtile cressant". I looked at some other books. They all had moons, but not all were crescent shaped and not all were green. Jenny had made hers full and yellow, Robyn had added stars for decoration. None of them knew what it was there for, and neither, at the time, did I. But I admired their handwork and they were pleased.

40

"We're not quite so dumb at social studies," said Heather, a pretty little brunette with dimples.

"I'm sure you're not dumb at all," I replied.

"We are but," said Lynn. "We're all dumb. We can't learn quick like the clever ones in C3A. That's why we have to take homecraft." She sighed deeply as she said this but continued to look perfectly happy.

"We've got a map to colour in," said Denise. "It's a real dag." She showed me a stamped map of Australia.

"Then you may colour it in this lesson," I said with relief.

For the rest of that period H3C cheerfully coloured in their maps. They coloured them purple, red, green, pink, and any other hue they could find or borrow. To improve the effect they drew more boundaries than the map provided – at random, anywhere at all, so that they could use more colours. The more boundaries, the more colours, and the more colours the prettier the map, so why stint them just for the sake of accuracy? A few of the more artistic inserted here and there for further decoration a bright blue river with a host of tributaries. They exchanged pencils with one another from time to time and were quite happy. When the bell rang I told them to finish their map for homework and to mark in the main towns. They looked at one another in surprise. Homework? "Gee, you're a dag!" remarked Denise.

Interval, and a cup of lukewarm tea. It was lukewarm because I had obeyed the First Assistant's instructions and stayed in my room until the class were all out. "Whatever for?" said Miss Harris. "No one else does."

"No one else is opposite Mr Good's office," replied Mrs Rose. "That room has more than one disadvantage."

After interval I was shown to the typing room, where I was to spend a double period with a fourth form, a class of thirty-two girls and one lone boy. The room was large and airy, the desks and typewriters were numbered, and each pupil apparently had an allotted desk, for they lost no time in going to their seats and uncovering their machines. There was no lack of interest here. Typing was evidently popular, and one of the girls played tuneful accompanying records on a small gramophone at the back of the room. It was very pleasant. The only incident occurred half-way through the first period, with the sudden opening of the door and the appearance of a young red-haired teacher whom I had already learned to be Miss Bailey. She ignored me and stamped angrily to the middle of the room. The typing ceased, as the pupils sensed better entertainment to come.

Miss Bailey stopped before a meek-looking, lank-haired girl.

"And *where*, Helen," she shouted, "is your bib?"

Helen said nothing.

"I warned you," said Miss Bailey. "I warned you I would check up today. Didn't I? Didn't I now? I warned you. I told you quite plainly that you would not be allowed to type if you didn't have it. Get out. Get OUT. Out, out, OUT."

Helen gathered up her things and walked slowly to the door, Miss Bailey following behind. She did not look at me, and the door slammed behind her.

The typewriters were still silent, and the class looking at me for my reaction to this interruption.

"What," I asked "is a bib?"

There was a general response. "This," said one girl as she pulled a piece of blue material out of her satchel. "This," said another and "This," said a third, as they reached for theirs. Another girl had gone to a cupboard against the far wall and was pulling out quantities of coloured squares. "Shall I give them out, Mrs Bream?"

"Whatever are they?"

The class laughed. "They're our bibs," they explained. "They fit on like this over our typewriters so we can't see what we're typing. See? Didn't you have one when you learned?" I had not learned typing at all, but thought it inadvisable to say so.

"No," I replied, "but it's a very good idea. Tell me, why was Helen told to leave for not having one? The rest of you were not using them either."

"Helen didn't *have* one," a girl explained. "She hadn't made one. Miss Bailey said she had to have one or she couldn't type any more. It's *having* one that really matters. We don't always use them."

I sensed a mild disapproval of my ignorance, a disapproval which remained with them all that term. A typing teacher who had never heard of a bib! They mistrusted me, and took all queries to Miss Bailey. But I didn't mind that. Typing periods seemed to run themselves, and apart from marking errors in their work and preventing peeking under bibs, my duties there were light and restful. The records which I had liked the first day grew less and less enjoyable as they were played period after period, but the children didn't seem to tire of them. Fortunately the shorthand teacher next door complained one day of the noise, and I was able to limit the records to one period a week.

After lunch, I returned to my own room, where another class soon lined up. By now I felt confident, experienced, and ten years older.

"Good afternoon, 3HTB." I tried to sound strong and masterful. "Come in please."

They did. They changed from a fairly order double row under the watchful eye of the First Assistant in his office over the way, to a herd of leaping, jostling bleating

43

sheep, trying to force their way through a three-foot gate. There was a fight among the boys to attain, and then to hold, a window seat. There was a scuffle, scraping of desks and feet, a chair overturned, a squeal of pain from a girl, shouts, rattles, case lids clacking. Then suddenly silence. They all looked at me. Someone had the idea of standing up, so all the class stood. And they looked at me again, those at the back craning to get a better view. I told them to sit, but this proved to be a complicated operation which lasted at least three minutes, with conversation and rearrangement of desks. If the boys found their position uncomfortable, they did not move their chair – they picked up their desk bodily and replaced it with a loud bang at an angle more convenient to them. But eventually all were settled and I noticed that their books were out. They didn't mind arithmetic. Their course – technical for the boys and homecraft for the girls – included core mathematics which aimed at giving them a limited, but practical, knowledge of essential calculations for future use. The textbook was well devised and the exercises realistic.

"Where are you up to in your book?" I asked a sandy-haired girl in the first row, as I took up my teacher's copy.

"Are you going to teach us all year?" was her reply.

"I think so. Now tell me what page you are up to."

"Chapter Six," called out a boy from the back.

"Chapter Seven," said the sandy-head in front.

There was promise of a lively argument, but I cut it short.

"We shall start at Chapter Six," I announced. "That will give you an opportunity to revise if you've already been through it and I shall be able to see how well you can do the work. All ready? Page forty-five. Look at the first exercise. Have you done this before? No? Then we'll

44

do it now. 'If a man smokes 60 cigarettes a week, will it pay him to buy them in packets of 20 for 1/6, or in boxes of 100 for 7/-?' "

There was silence.

"Come on – what do you think?" I addressed a lively looking boy.

"I dunno."

"It's silly," said a blonde by the window.

Another pause. "How do you do it?" asked a boy.

"You work out how much he will spend each way and find out which way is cheaper for him. Try it in your books."

No one moved. "It's silly," said the blonde again. "Why would he buy 100 cigarettes if he only smokes 60?" There was a murmur of approval at this. I explained the advantages of bulk buying, I did the exercise on the board, and I passed on to the next, which I read aloud.

"If you go to a grocer's shop and see two tins of peas . . . "

"Huh! Housework!" said a boy in disgust.

"Be quiet. 'If you go to a grocer's shop and see two tins of peas, one of 8 oz. for 1/6 and one of 16 oz. for 2/10 . . .' "

A hand went up.

"I don't *like* tinned peas. I wouldn't get them. Frozen ones are nicer."

"They are not," said her neighbour, without bothering to put up her hand first. "The frozen ones taste funny. I like tinned ones better."

There was a brief discussion by the girls on the relative merits of tinned or frozen peas. I suddenly thought of dried ones, and intervened before anyone could bring them in to complicate matters further.

"Frozen peas are unprocurable," I said quickly. "There is a shortage and you just have to have peas.

45

Your *husband* likes peas," I added, as a hand went up.
I felt sure she was about to recommend beans instead.
"Now you go to the grocer's and you see two tins . . . "

The lesson continued. We made a decision about the
peas, and passed on to carpet of six foot and twelve
foot widths.

I never found out why 3HTB enjoyed arithmetic. It
was, next to typing, my easiest class that year. They
didn't like "silly" questions, which demanded thought
and decisions, for which they were ill equipped, but when
they understood and approved the questions asked,
they were quite attentive. The simpler exercises they
carried out almost with enthusiasm. They particularly
liked adding up four-figure numbers, and at the end of
each term they willingly balanced my register for me –
a task at which they were more competent than I.

They ruled off each exercise with a red pen and they
took a pride in keeping their books neat. As long as I
kept them busy and did not demand too much understanding from them at one time, they were happy and
relatively good. I introduced new work very slowly and
gently, and they made marked progress during the year.
Of course there were some who did not even like
arithmetic, and sought other diversions during the lesson,
but they were fewer in this class than in any other except
typing. I liked 3HTB.

A School Certificate form filed in next for a period of
English. There are few creatures more conservative,
hide-bound, and mentally inflexible, than a fifth form
secondary pupil. Third and fourth-formers are receptive
to what interests them, however little that may be, and
to the limit of their intelligence they will criticise,
protest, argue, and investigate, what you have to say.
Whether it is a new concept for them or an orthodox
restatement of what they have already heard, is im-

material. They argue on principle. Sixth-formers are beginning to think for themselves and to question the statements of both teachers and textbooks – a very healthy stage. But the fifth-former resents any interference with his little tied-up package of set ideas and values. He doesn't know this – he thinks he is progressive and daring. What is fashionable among teenagers, is right, and what is good enough for the Beatles is good enough for him. But fashion is something decreed for him, and not by him – he makes no innovations and is frightened by them. As far as his school work goes, this attitude is on the whole a handicap. The first statement to gain access to the unoccupied paddocks of his mind is the one he accepts. Others which conflict with it are trespassers to be evicted without hearing. Getting any fact into those empty paddocks is itself a hard task for a school-teacher in many cases, and if the gate happens to be open when you make a slip of the tongue, or a mistake of fact, the damage is almost irreparable. For it is one of the great natural laws in the science of teaching that if there is one incorrect statement in a comprehensive, learned exposition of any subject, a pupil will notice it, read it, absorb it, and retain it for months on end. With nonchalant ease he spots all the misprints, misspellings, and outdated theories in a textbook and commits them firmly to memory.

5HTB had been taught English for two months by an expert in technical drawing. He had not wanted to teach English, he had protested that he was quite incapable of teaching English, and he had then made a thorough and a fully conscientious effort to teach English. It was certainly not his fault that the finer points of syntax, figures of speech and prosody at times eluded him. But it made my progress with 5HTB more difficult.

The first obstruction occurred in this lesson. They told me they had been studying verse forms, so I wrote the names of a few simple ones on the board – ode, ballad, sonnet . . .

"Ballade is spelt with an 'e' on the end," said one of the boys.

"Not this sort," I explained. "Ballade with an 'e' is a French form of verse and a different thing altogether. The one you have to know about is b-a-l-l-a-d, *Sir Patrik Spens, The Ancient Mariner*, and so on."

"But *The Ancient Mariner* is a ballade with an 'e'. Mr Tozer gave us notes on it. There you are." He opened his book.

"You must have copied it down wrongly from the board," I said.

An earnest-looking girl spoke up. "No, it *is* spelt with an 'e', Mrs Bream. I've got it that way too."

"So have I."

"So have I."

"It's in the dictionary with an 'e'."

"Both forms should be in the dictionary," I said. "Mr Tozer was either referring to the French form, or else he absentmindedly put an 'e' on the end without thinking. It's so easy to do that."

There were mutterings of disbelief, disapproval and resentment. I emphasised my point. I explained the rhyme and stanza scheme of ballad and ballade, and the difference between them. I spent some time on it before passing on to the sonnet. Before the lesson ended I reminded them again of the correct spelling, and the next morning I recapitulated. It was an essential part of their syllabus, and I wanted no mistake. Yet at the end of a week when I gave a test, *The Ancient Mariner* was referred to by all except five of them as a ballade. It was not that they trusted one teacher more than another. It was simply a matter of which teacher made the first statement on any subject. This made conversation awkward with them, for I had to take great care with my words. I knew that if I accidentally made an inaccurate statement on any subject, from horses to helicopters, they would remember it, believe it, and reproduce it to other teachers with the unanswerable proof that "Mrs Bream told us so."

Another major problem in teaching the fifth form was that it was a mixed class, and my lessons had to compete with the far more lively interest which my pupils took in one another. An enforced segregation of girls and boys in the playground stimulated their social ambitions in the classroom, and learning had to give way to a far more powerful natural urge. What chance had adjectival clauses against Gavin's curly mop of black hair or Ellen's large blue eyes?

5HTB was not an easy class to teach, and, like nearly all School Certificate forms, its members held their final examination in such remote disregard at this time of the year, that it provided almost no incentive to work. When you're sixteen and it's still summer, the end of the year is a long way off.

My last class of the day was 4HTB whom I was to take for English. They were noisy and restless and promised to be troublesome. For this period I was a novelty to them and they listened to me, but I foresaw correctly that they would be a difficult form to control. They did not like English, they did not like school, and they particularly disliked last periods in the afternoon of a hot day. They had one ambition – to turn fifteen and leave school. After twenty minutes' struggle on my part to keep their attention, and on theirs to resist any accidental infiltration of literary or grammatical knowledge, a girl put up her hand.

49

"Yes, Barbara?" I had learned her name early in the lesson, through her refusal to stop talking.

"I'm going to faint."

She was pink-cheeked and looked healthily robust – quite unlike any about-to-faint person I had ever encountered.

"Don't be so silly," I snapped. "Get on with your work."

"She probably is, Mrs Bream," said a boy. "She does." She did. There and then. Her pink cheeks changed with alarming suddenness to a pasty yellow, and she slipped in a heap off her chair onto the floor. I had not yet been shown where the sick room was, or told the procedure to follow in cases such as this, and I felt unreasonably angry with Barbara as I marched down the aisle. What right had she to faint in my first lesson with the class? And on my first teaching day? She could have waited until next week, or done it in someone else's room. The other pupils were unperturbed and not even particularly interested. I asked a girl to fetch some water, I placed a blazer under Barbara's head, and when she had recovered enough, I sent her with two companions to the sick room. Doubtless they knew where to find it. I sent another pupil to inform Miss Ferguson, who would surely be in charge of such matters. But when I located the sick room after the lesson, Barbara was no longer there. I found her out with her friends, talking lustily and preparing to go home. After that Barbara fainted in my class on an average of at least once a fortnight. She usually had the courtesy to tell me first, and in time I would just leave her in the aisle until she came to, stepping over her as I conducted the lesson. Miss Ferguson told me that her parents were quite unconcerned about Barbara's frequent fainting spells – they had taken her to a doctor who said she would "just grow out of it." This sounded odd to me, but I suppose he knew, and Barbara at least was unworried. She said that she "didn't mind fainting", that she never felt sick or unwell before or afterwards. She just knew she was going to, and it wasn't unpleasant. I suspected in fact that she had learned to make the most of this unusual gift, and could bring on a faint at will, because one often followed hot on an awkward question by me concerning homework not done, or unexplained absence from class. It was a useful accomplishment, which the rest of her form rather envied.

"Not as bad as I expected," I told my colleagues at afternoon tea. "Well, not as bad as you led me to believe. It's just different somehow. Not what I thought."

"The first day is always the best," laughed Mrs Rose. "You're something new to them; you hold their interest for a while; and some of them hope you haven't talked to the other teachers yet, so that they can impress you. Wait a little – it won't last."

She was right. As my classes became gradually familiar with my appearance, my clothes, the mole on my cheek, my manner of speaking and my habit of tossing a piece of chalk in my left hand, they grew bored and reverted to making their own amusement. Even my white hair and my undeserved reputation for being "very high up" failed to be a deterrent to misbehaviour, because it brought no dire retribution with it. Indeed retribution of the dire variety was hard to devise. I felt myself caught up in the struggle which brings frustration to nearly all teachers – the struggle against unwillingness to learn, against hostility to authority and discipline, against overcrowded classrooms, and against an un-reasonable ban by the Education Department on leg chains and horse whips.

The children were on the whole appallingly lazy, they

51

lacked direction and self-control, they were obstinate and wilful. I learned that they came from the poorest districts of the city. Some of the High Schools in the town selected their pupils with care – the Boys' High School had a waiting list for which either brains or a brother was said to be the qualification. Some other schools – the more tolerant -- worked on the zoning system, taking as new pupils only those living within a certain radius of the school. But the headmaster here accepted anyone. Some he enrolled were those rejected by, or expelled from, other schools, and nearly all were from poor homes. He never refused a pupil, and the prestige of his school seemed entirely subordinate to his concern for the welfare of the children who needed schooling. I admired him greatly for this, as for many other out-standing qualities. He was an exceptionally fine and upright character, and I was glad to be working under the direction of such a man.

It would be nice to add that he was patient, even-tempered and self-controlled. But this is doubtful. With a roll of over nine hundred and fifty children, a constant staff shortage (owing not only to the wide-spread dearth of teachers but to the reputation of our pupils for being rough and refractory) and a Scottish temperament, he was reputed to fly into violent rages with staff, parents, or pupils alike. His secretary, a delightful little middle-aged woman with grey hair and a happy disposition, acted as barometer of his temper pressure. It was the common practice to ring down to Mrs Lane before attempting to see the headmaster on any matter.

"Good morning, Mrs Lane," a teacher would say. "Do you think it will be fine today?"

"There's rain coming up," she would reply, or "It's very pleasant just now," or "I heard thunder this morning, but it may have passed over."

I never used this method myself, not through confidence or bravado, but simply because I didn't know about it for several months, nor of the existence of the Principal's renowned temper. He spoke quietly and calmly in assembly, he swayed gently and rhythmically onto his toes during the hymns, and he gave the appearance of being utterly self-possessed and calm. The hall of nearly a thousand pupils was always amazingly quiet during his presence on the stage, and this in itself should have made me suspect that he had some unknown gifts with which to control or intimidate, but I did not suspect a display of wrath as one of them. One thing did puzzle me in assembly – his delightful Scottish accent pronounced many commonly short 'a's as long ones, yet there was not a murmur or snigger when he referred during the Bible reading to Balaam "sitting on his ass." The soberness with which the school received this statement was indicative of his discipline and the awe with which the pupils regarded him.

I never saw his temper in action. It is still in fact only a rumour to me, and may not have existed at all. He greeted me courteously and patiently each time I went to his office, and listened tolerantly to every query. He never hurried me, however busy he was, and he offered friendly and very wise advice on my problems. Yet he was reputed to have thrown a telephone directory at the history master, and to have boxed many a girl's ears. The staff were afraid of him, and fortunately the pupils were too. The ultimate resort was then to send a pupil to the Principal for punishment. But this was done only when all else failed, not only out of consideration for the Principal, whose day was overfull of administration problems, but because we all regarded it as an admission of defeat. Defeated we usually were, but not often ready to admit it.

53

Chapter 4

Discipline was my preoccupation for the next few months, and indeed it is the first concern of every teacher. I discovered, however, that it is a tricky subject to raise. Staff are rather touchy about their discipline. You can criticise another teacher's methods of presenting work, his speech, his appearance, his marking, his material, his industry, without giving offence. But you must never cast a slight on his discipline. "Control" they call it. We newer teachers found a common bond in our lack of control, but we too were a little sensitive about the deficiency. In moments of weakness we would sometimes admit our difficulties and exchange confidences, but not openly in the staffroom – rather in a dark corner of the library or behind the door of an unused classroom. There we would confess our failure. We were drawn together in misfortune, and it was comforting, even if humiliating, to compare experiences.

"I told Heather McRobb that she was late for class," said Miss Burton. "She threw all her books in the air and said 'Aw you go and get lost!' Then she walked out and I haven't seen her since. What should I do?"

"We don't know. What *did* you do?"

"I made one of the other girls pick up her books and

put them in a neat pile on the table. It didn't seem quite adequate to the occasion."

"No, I guess not. You'll have to take some decisive action, won't you?"

"Yes. Just what decisive action had you in mind?"

We didn't have any. The demand for decisive actions always seemed to be outrunning the supply.

"Take her to Miss Ferguson, I suppose," said Mrs Rose.

"Poor Miss Ferguson. And anyway, the other day I did tell Miss Ferguson about Heather's habitual lateness for class and said I thought something ought to be done about it. Miss Ferguson smiled nicely and said yes, she quite agreed, and I was the one to do it. She was quite right, of course. I know that. But what *can* I do?"

"Don't let her back into the room."

"The last time I kept her out she went down to the toilets, put the plug in a basin and turned the tap on full, then came back and stood quietly outside my door again. At least I could bet it was her. The caretaker was furious – the whole cloakroom was swimming in water and some of the satchels were soaked through."

We couldn't help. "Just hope she never returns," said Mrs Rose. "After all she didn't actually swear at you. Last week I told a girl to read and she replied 'I bloody well won't. You just try and make me.'"

"Well whatever did *you* do?"

"I couldn't let a thing like that pass. I marched her straight down to Miss Ferguson. I was scared she wouldn't come, but she did. Like a lamb. I left her with Miss Ferguson, because I had to get back to the class and stop them from wrecking the chairs – or each other – and when she came back she had obviously been crying. She's been quite polite and good ever since. What does Miss Ferguson do to them?"

56

"She doesn't do anything to them except talk. What else is there to do?"

"The real trouble," said Mrs Rose, "is that we have no effective form of punishment. If we could only play nonchalantly with a long steel ruler, or point to our notes with a firm springy length of bamboo . . . "

"I did," I told her. "Mr Hercus took a class in my room and left his cane behind. I used it for indicating places on a wall map, and I tapped it menacingly on my table. Then Gail McNaught borrowed it to get her pencil out from under the heater."

"It's not so bad with the boys," said Miss Burton. "You can have someone use the cane on them. Mr Good's always willing."

"But caning just doesn't work with some of the boys. They collect canings, like scout badges or postage stamps. It puts them in good with the girls. There's a kind of competition among the bad ones to try to get more than their friends. They compare stripes and put notches on their rulers. Mooney of 4 Ag. had them all down each side of his, Mr Bowron says. He couldn't make out why all Mooney's ruled lines were so regularly wiggly – made his geometry book look most peculiar. Then Mr Bowron confiscated the ruler and Mooney was terribly upset."

"That gives Mr Bowron a terrific hold on him until he gives it back."

"Yes, he says Mooney begs for it every day and is behaving like an angel."

"At least caning is a real punishment for some of the boys. They don't *all* enjoy it. And you feel you've done something if you have them caned. You haven't let them walk over you, and it shows them that you mean business. But there must be other ways."

"Mr Newall doesn't have any trouble when he takes a class."

57

"He's the headmaster. He's surrounded by a sort of gleaming aura which protects him like an electric fence."

"Mr Good manages all right too."

"He has a lesser aura, being the deputy head. And he's got a cane. And he shouts. And he's old. Oh I don't know – he just does it somehow."

"So does Miss Ferguson. And she doesn't shout. But her classes are always quiet."

"That's true."

We decided that there must be a secret which no one had yet revealed to us, a magic key to discipline, and we asked other teachers for the answer, without, of course, admitting that we found any great difficulty ourselves. We had our pride too. Other teachers were most willing to help and gave us ready advice. They told us it was confidence, they told us that the children "just knew" when they couldn't get away with it, they smiled smugly and pityingly and told us it would come to us with time. Miss Bailey even offered to take Miss Burton's class for her one day, and "teach them how to behave", a suggestion which made Miss Burton rather angry. But we listened gratefully to all of their other suggestions. Then one of us saw a boy climbing out of Mr Howe's window while he was conducting a social studies class. We heard the din from Mr Robertson's mathematics group, we looked through the glass panel while Miss Bailey was taking shorthand. And we didn't ask teachers for advice any more.

It was confidence, I decided. An air of assurance and a friendly, positive approach. Like dogs. They smell you when you are afraid, I had heard. So approach with confidence and trust. Offer the hand of friendship and they will lick it with gratitude. Well, I approached with confidence. I oozed trust and assurance. But my pupils didn't seem to know about dogs. When I offered the hand of friendship they closed their gleeful little fangs on it and drank my blood. It simply didn't work.

Then I tried the gentle, kindly approach. That didn't work either. When I smiled with sweet motherliness they decided that I was "in a good mood" and that they could get away with more misbehaviour than usual. When I said untruthfully, "Now I know that you are really a good class", they roared with laughter and set about seeing how quickly they could prove me wrong.

I tried the hypnotic eye. I aimed at looking inscrutable and calm, and exuding an inner power. I practised on the cat one night, and he went to sleep, so I knew there must be something in it. I stared fixedly at one class and said in a compelling tone, "Now this period there will be no talking from you, and no shuffling of chairs." This was received with a grin of sheer disbelief and an ironical jeer from the back row. Then they all talked and shuffled their chairs.

After a few weeks my womanliness had withered into desiccated little shreds, and even these seemed to be dropping from me. I felt mean, surly, embittered, warped and twisted. I was developing a desire for revenge which I could never remember having felt before since my early infant school days when a small boy held my new book under the drinking fountain. I wanted a cane, I wanted a stinging cane, one with little prickles on it, no – nails perhaps, nails that would tear the flesh and make blood run and elicit agonised screams of pain and cries for mercy.

"That's cruel," said Mrs Donning. "I'd rather have an epidemic. An infantile one, of course, so that we wouldn't get it ourselves. One that rages through the school and keeps them all at home. Not serious, but very infectious and prolonged. Six weeks' isolation at least."

"You'd lose your job," said Mrs Rose. "They'd do

59

correspondence lessons through the newspapers and we wouldn't be required."

"I'll give it just two more months," said Miss Burton. "Then I'll resign. I really will. I need the money too badly just now. But it's not worth it. I can't sleep, my cheek twitches, I jump at sudden noises and I'm not fit to live in a house with other people – my family tell me so nearly every evening."

"You should just hear me now when I go into a shop," sighed Miss Harris. "I used to be quite nice to the shop assistants. I would say humbly 'Good morning. Would you mind seeing whether you have a card of small safety pins? Thank you so much.' Yesterday I asked for some wool to match a sample I had, and do you know I only just stopped myself from adding 'and hurry up about it'? And then when they couldn't match the sample I felt quite cross with them – as though they had failed to carry out an exercise I had set for homework."

"Yes, teaching does have a terrible effect on your character – it develops the worst in you and gives you nothing noble in exchange."

"Mrs Bream, have you ever heard Mr Good taking morning assembly?"

Yes, I had, and I knew what she meant. In Mr Newall's absence one day Mr Good had given the Bible reading and led the Lord's Prayer. He had certainly not meant to be irreverent, but he had rapped out "Give us this day our daily bread" in a tone of curt, incisive command, and when he had finished, I almost expected him to add "and kindly see to it that all these matters are completed without fail before morning interval!"

I soon decided that the acquisition of control would come, if at all, only with experience, and could apparently be achieved by individual means which varied with each teacher.

There was the sort based on prestige, or position. This belonged exclusively to the Principal and the First Assistant.

There was that gained by intimidation. Mr Rowlings had this. He overwhelmed any resistance by a torrent of noise and strength and physical superiority. Of course this worked only with the boys. Others who taught boys relied on constant caning, or on the convenience of the daily punishment queue outside Mr Good's study door. Miss McComish, the cooking teacher, also contrived to keep her girls not exactly in abject fear of her, but fairly well subdued, by her good-natured blustering manner, her own physical size, and an indefatigable vigilance. They seldom defied Miss Mc-Comish, because they had a good idea that if they waged battle, she would come off best.

Miss Tulley, too, had the upper hand by a more moderate use of the same methods. But both she and Miss McComish taught practical subjects, in which most of the girls were genuinely interested.

There was another sort of control, brought about by the personality of the teacher. The Senior Mistress, Miss Ferguson, had this in its best shape. She never raised her voice. She spoke gently and entirely without venom, and yet as she walked down the corridor the less amenable children fled before her advancing footsteps. She never seemed to punish severely or upbraid scathingly. Perhaps even the diabolical spirit of the worst schoolgirl could discern the gentle sincerity of her purpose and her submission to her vocation. For her it was obviously a vocation, not a job. Perhaps the brighter among them were also quelled in part by their perception of her delightful sense of humour, which could enjoy

61

without a sneer the situations in which her position involved her. Of course her dominion did not extend beyond the girls. Nor was her discipline perfect – whose is? She was faced with the occasional defiance, insolence and refusal to conform or obey. But her classes on the whole were quiet and contented, and those pupils reported to her by angry teachers were usually the better for their visit.

Another personal type of control belonged to one of the science masters, Mr Lockhead. He wore a permanent sneer when in front of a class. He seldom meted out punishment other than verbal abuse, but this was withering, cutting, and interlaced with that unkindest of all classroom repressive measures, sarcasm. The children detested him and behaved for him. Long before I thought of teaching I had resolved never to resort to sarcasm with any child. It is a measure possessing no constructive merit at all. It wounds without curing, it destroys without building, and it is, moreover, a most unfair weapon for any adult to use against a child who is ill-equipped both in intelligence and in opportunity, to retaliate. Mr Lockhead was one of the nicest, most generous men I had ever met, and this side of his teaching puzzled me. He did much for his pupils which they never guessed at, and were never told, and his examination results were among the best in the school. But I had no desire to imitate his methods.

Then there was voice. Just voice. This, of course, is almost entirely a masculine attribute, although Miss McComish could increase the volume of her tones in a way which the rest of the women envied. In spite of what the First Assistant had told me, I realised that even the noisiest pupils will submit to a being who can shout just a little more loudly than they can. (This doubtless explains the popularity of some of the singing groups of today.) In a modified form, some women teachers can use voice as an aid. You can develop a musical, resonant, interesting voice with such variety of accent and tone and cadence that it holds your class's attention whenever you speak – so I have been told. I have not yet heard one like that among school teachers. Or you can make the most of the voice you happen to have. By lowering it until your pupils have to strain to hear you, then suddenly raising it in a fortissimo of fury, a certain surprise and alarm can be produced. Shock tactics. But that stratagem was not for me. I tried it once. My form was not used to it from me, and after the first surprise they leaned back and giggled with delight. The next morning there were several enquiries after my health. They did hope I felt better – gee, I had got upset yesterday. I have never done it since, but I am told that it can be effective.

Then there's the Man Next Door, in my case Mr Bowron. Being a man, he had the privilege of wielding a cane, and sending a boy to Mr Bowron, who helped me out as a comrade, was not the humiliating experience of having to send one to Mr Good or to the Principal. Nor, unfortunately, was it as effective. But I could take a boy to Mr Bowron with the knowledge that he would not cane him unless he considered it really desirable. He was well practised in verbal lashing too, so I could send girls to him also if I wished.

The other women told me that I was very lucky in having the First Assistant just over the passage from my room. But the position did nothing to help me.

The first period after assembly each day was reserved by Mr Good for punishing malefactors. They lined up outside the door of his office, with various expressions of boredom or anticipation, and would disappear one by one into the sanctum. If the door was shut after them,

63

the prognosis was bad. In my room just opposite, the whack of the cane could be clearly heard. If I then looked through the glass portion of my door, the rest of the queue would grin cheerfully at me, and sometimes put up their fingers to indicate the number of cuts the offender had just received.

"You won't have any trouble at all with the boys," the staff assured me. "All you need do to frighten them is to put one or two in the caning queue in the corridor outside your room. They will realise how easy it is for you to do that when you're so close."

This sounded quite right in theory, but in practice . . . well, I tried it.

"The next boy who calls out in class," I said resolutely to 3HTB, "will be sent over to Mr Good." The next boy who called out was a small, curly-haired, wide-eyed child called John Herrin. I angrily put him at the end of the queue which had already been formed – it was the first period of the day. Then I walked up and down my bench, trying to conduct the lesson. It had certainly been an effective measure. The class was now quiet and attentive, and no one else called out. But time passed slowly; I began to have doubts. I looked through the glass – the queue was still long. I continued the lesson, but kept being interrupted by visions of the diminutive Herrin bending over a chair. I looked again. The queue had begun to move on – it was noticeably shorter, and Herrin looked frightened. At last I could stand it no longer. I could not bring Herrin back into the classroom, because that would destroy all vestige of my authority over this form, but perhaps I could prevent the actual caning. I abandoned the class and stopped the First Assistant as he was ushering in the next of his victims. He was not pleased. This was a daily ritual at which he did not favour any interruption. I almost pushed him back into his office, and said, "I've put a little boy at the end of the queue, but don't cane him. Please don't cane him."

The First Assistant looked at me coldly.

"I'll cane whom I please," he stated. He seemed very angry. I tried to explain, I remonstrated, I pleaded, while he impatiently tapped his cane on the desk at intervals, and looked very much as if he would have liked to invite me to bend over myself. He let me talk for five minutes. At the end of that time he informed me with a rather amused twinkle that he never did cane first-years anyway – well, not until the third or fourth offence. And in due course Herrin returned unabashed, and in answer to the questioning eyebrows of his friends across the room, called out happily, "Nothink. Nothink at all." I realised that this was a course which was not going to aid me and I gave it up.

I had thought at first that the caning queue would even help to subdue the girls, that they would have a constant sobering thought that there, but for the grace of their sex, went they. But it was just the reverse. My girls enjoyed the existence of the caning queue. They revelled in it. On any change of timetable they looked eagerly to see how often they came to my room for the first period of the day. The queue provided more boys to make faces at while they lined up for class, and if they were lucky they might see some of their current boy friends there, and be able to exchange a few words. When they heard the whacks they merely looked smug and happy at this reminder of their immunity from corporal punishment, and it gave them another subject to discuss with their neighbours during my lesson.

For girls, the field of retribution is sadly limited. You can rebuke them verbally. You can give them a dissertation on their crimes, their weakness, and the probably

65

unpleasant future which is awaiting them round the corner if they continue in their present state of lamentable gracelessness. This can be done either publicly, before their classmates, or in a tête-à-tête after the lesson. In either case I found that I ran out of words in the first few minutes. I have seen and envied teachers who kept their victim squirming for a quarter of an hour or longer, but I have never found out what they said in all that time, or how they managed to keep speaking without exhausting their ideas. It seemed effective enough in others; it was no good to me.

You can appeal to their better nature and their finer feelings, to their sense of justice and of live-and-let-live. I seldom attempted this. It seemed below the belt in a good clean fight, and moreover I doubted its efficacy. If they had finer feelings, they were certainly not going to have me playing around on them, not, at least, at this early stage of my teaching career. I was fair game, and expected to recognise this fact, and not mess about with the rules of the contest. I knew instinctively that I would get nowhere with the "Come now, ... " tactics.

Lines? I remembered the "lines bank" which my son and his friends had kept at their primary school in one of my discarded shoe boxes. All neatly sorted into matching ink and printing. You paid two hundred lines as entrance fee, and they were then available to you whenever your need for them arose during the year. This scheme was made possible by an obliging teacher who threw them untorn into the wastepaper basket, from where it was easy to retrieve them after school and return them to the bank for future use. I did not really suspect these girls of such organisation among themselves, and I would certainly make sure that I destroyed their efforts, but even so I could never be quite sure that lines set to be done out of school hours would be completed by the actual culprit. Besides, what sort of lines could be set? Repetitive lines are usually a complete waste of time, and must have a frustrating, not reformative, effect on an intelligent pupil. I could hardly blame a girl, after writing "I must not scribble on the desk" two hundred times, for inscribing the two hundred and first effort on the wall. Lines of their textbook, or copied notes, could perhaps be more useful. But these had to be carefully chosen so that the punishment did not damn with premature distaste any subject or written matter which might possibly hold interest for them later. It would be criminal to subject Shakespeare or any cherished author to such indignity, and even history textbooks deserved a better fate. No doubt somebody loved them. I must choose something too dull to be de-souled by the process, yet useful in its facts. A page or two of the dictionary was usually my choice, but I still thought it was rather tough on the little *Pocket Oxford* which was issued to the pupils. It is not a completely dull work by any means, nor devoid of character.

Instead of lines, exercises could be set, or essays. But to be of any use, these had to be corrected later. Moreover, setting work of any kind to be done at home was too hopeful. We could keep the offender in school at interval or at lunch time, but to do this effectively we must stay in ourselves, and interval and lunch hours are breaks more precious and necessary to the teacher than to the pupil. I also found that on a cold day in winter I was sometimes conferring a benefit on a naughty pupil who remained inside, leisurely copying out a passage, or writing an essay, by the heater, while her better-behaved friends shivered in the cheerless concrete playground outside.

There was organised detention. This was held every

67

day after school, and supervised by the teachers on duty. The woman duty teacher was always required, because girls' and boys' detentions were held in separate rooms. This was not only advisable, but necessary, as both rooms were always full to overflowing. It was easy enough to give a detention. You simply entered the name in a special book, recorded the offence – such as "throwing books out of the window", "sticking gum on the bannister", "removing the leg of a school desk", "fighting in the corridor" – then you signed your own name, dated the entry, and that was that. But the more who attended detention, the more inconvenience and worry for the duty teacher. And when pupils who were entered in the detention book failed to attend, the task of enquiring into their absence usually fell ultimately onto Miss Ferguson or Mr Good. Naturally teachers who made a habit of using the detention book did not top the poll for popularity.

One could, of course, report girls to Miss Ferguson, the Principal, or to any senior teacher who could perhaps subdue them. This was a last resort, and we were in fact reminded at times that the discipline of our classes was our own responsibility. It was suggested once by a visiting inspector that a good scheme for suppressing a particularly troublesome pupil was a concentrated one-day effort on the part of teachers. By arrangement they all, on the same day, should successively report the offender to the same senior member of staff, the idea being, I think, that even if the pupil's nerves could stand it, those of the senior teacher would most certainly crack under the strain, and his resultant final outburst would have all the freshness and force of a violent unpremeditated eruption. We did not adopt this idea. The cold-blooded planning of it, like an army manoeuvre, emphasised to us the unnatural relationship

68

which existed between most of the pupils and ourselves. We had to recognise the fact that we were two opposing camps, but we all at heart preferred to aim for honourable peace, rather than successful warfare.

The crowning punishment for girls, short of actual expulsion, was considered to be suspension for a period from school. Board approval had to be obtained before this could be carried out, so it was not recommended lightly. Nor was it always done to good effect, because suspension was sometimes enjoyed by the malefactor as an unexpected and welcome holiday. If parents were kind, it could be a more pleasant week than one spent at school. Cheryl, one of my pupils in 4HTB, came back from suspension glowing with health and joy. She told me she had spent a glorious ten days with her aunt in Nelson. " . . . and Auntie said 'Do come again, dear. Try to get some more time off before the end of the year.' " Luckily the comic side of this was not lost on Cheryl, who was quite a likeable child, and Auntie did not have her company again that year. But others, more hardened, would wander about the town with their parents' consent, and the taste of freedom did little to improve their attitude towards school discipline and authority. If parents were not kind, the Board doubtless hesitated to inflict suspension. I was shown the weals on a girl's legs after a week of this punishment, and the only noticeable difference in her subsequent behaviour was the addition of resentment and a surly frown which had not been present before.

My own form, H3C, were relatively good for me; that is, their conduct was noticeably better than it was in most other rooms. They did not squirt ink at me or use me as a target in disposing of their deflavoured chewing gum, and for this I was grateful. They obeyed me generally, in their own good time, though largely through good nature and not deference. They were not defiant, and they kept reasonably quiet for most of my lessons. Beyond this point, I could not improve their behaviour. It was not for want of trying.

"Talk to them," said Mr Bowron. "Just talk to them. It works. Tell them how bad they are and what will happen to them one day. You know – the fate of the criminal in modern society – bring in manhunts and lynching and ostracism and poverty – point out what they're heading towards. Threaten them, persuade them. Talk to them like that for ten minutes at the beginning of the period. You just try it – it really works."

He did not teach H3C, but I was ready to give anything a go.

The next lesson began in the usual way. "Come in, girls," I said. "Quietly, QUIETLY . . . sit down. Jenny, turn round – Margaret, stop talking – Shirley, we're waiting for you – Susan!! – never mind that truck outside the window, Heather – Beverley, your attention please – pick that up at once, Denise – Sheila, leave Diane alone – Diane, no talking – you are NOT to call out, Carolyn . . . " As I said, it began in the usual way. And as usual they gave me a few brief and not unfriendly glances, then continued to do as they liked. In a moment of accidental silence, I tapped the blackboard duster on the table. I seldom did this, as I dislike chalk dust. It was a new sound, they all looked at me, and I began.

I listed their faults (the minor ones – some were not fit for public airing), I mentioned punishments which awaited them in school if they did not mend their ways, I gave an account of the horrible retribution which might overtake them in later years. I deplored their attitude, their disobedience, their slovenly appearance, their manners. Then I saw to my surprise that I had their full attention. This time, I told myself, I was really

70

achieving something. I was making my presence felt. I warmed up to my subject, and continued my speech with vigour, ignoring Denise's hand which kept flapping at me from the front row. I went on talking, as Mr Bowron had advised. I made myself quite clear. I told them just what I expected from them in future. Jenny's hand was up too. "In a minute, Jenny," I interrupted. "Put your hand down for now." Jenny put her hand down for a minute, then raised it and continued a slow waving. All eyes were still on me, so I made the most of this unusual attention. There were several more hands up soon, but I took no notice. I spoke for another few minutes, to make sure I had omitted nothing, and to repeat those phrases and threats which I thought had been particularly telling; then, with a pleasing feeling of satisfaction, I rounded off my speech: " . . . And so in future I shall expect much better behaviour from all you girls. And now, Jenny, what is it?"

"Mrs Bream," said Jenny gently, "you have left your comb sticking in your hair."

I gathered together the remnants of my dignity and removed the comb. The class gave me a friendly smile, as if implying that they often did the same thing themselves, and resumed their former conversation and activities. Heather turned her eyes back to the truck outside the window, Pamela swung round to examine the picture on the back wall, Colleen continued to deepen the groove she was making in her neighbour's desk with a compass, and Hazel reached across the aisle to snatch a key from Yvonne.

Chapter 5

There were two weekly events which were particularly disliked by the women staff, mainly because of the dreary regularity with which they arrived, and could be expected, each week. Other occasions may have been worse in fact; these had the added discomfort of anticipation and inevitability.

One was the sports afternoon. I had at first looked forward to this, thinking it would be pleasant to move about in the open air and to take some welcome exercise myself as I supervised the children. I pictured myself running vigorously up and down the sideline of a hockey field, shouting encouragement to the losing side and offering hints on technique and strategy to both teams, who would be hotly contesting the issue. In later years and at subsequent schools, this has frequently been the case. Sports periods can be, and often are, a delightful break from school routine, and the enthusiasm of the pupils is infectious and relaxing. A good time is had by all. But at this school most of the girls had a strange distaste for all forms of organised physical activity. Perhaps they took sufficient exercise during lesson periods, where they wriggled, shuffled and fidgeted continually. Whatever their reason, they showed an abhorrence of physical education periods, of marching in columns and of supervised sport. Not all, of course, were affected this way. There were some enthusiastic girls who represented the school in teams, and were eager for any practice they could have, but these more promising players were naturally not entrusted to the care of newcomers among the teachers. They were taken separately to isolated areas for coaching and the rest of us saw little of them in action.

The last two periods on Thursday afternoon were those allotted to sport. Most of us were assigned to softball in summer and basketball in winter, and most of us knew nothing about either, having played tennis and hockey only. This was a minor setback, as books of rules were quickly produced. The main difficulty was that owing to the inadequacy of the small, paved playground, we used for our sports afternoon one of the public parks, a mile and a half away from the school. The pupils walked or cycled to the park, the staff in charge accompanying or following close behind, and trying to steer them there like so many good earnest sheep dogs. One of us went first – usually Miss McComish, who was in charge – others took the side streets, some the rear, all of us trying to intercept the would-be escapees who hoped to make full use of this golden opportunity. The prefects were told to walk down with those who had no bicycles, but prefects were easy to evade. The cyclists had better opportunity still. They could quickly and unexpectedly turn into a side street, from where they could pedal off home, or to the town, to indulge in sports for which we did not cater in the park. At times they would meet us head on, which was an interesting situation. Some would attempt to look confused and lost, and the fact that they had lived in the city all their young lives would not prevent them from saying, "Oh . . . is *that* the way? We weren't quite sure." Others would be going back for their sandshoes, or trying to find their friends. Some even expressed concern that they had not seen us, and described how they had turned back to make sure we were on the way.

We herded as many as we could into the park, and when the heeler teachers had arrived, we marked the rolls. This in itself was quite a big operation in a large park with over four hundred girls to account for. There were always absentees, whose names had to be carefully noted. They were shared out fairly, each teacher being responsible during the coming week for pursuing and persecuting those on her list. When we caught up with them the absentees would usually swear that they had been present, and their friends would readily confirm this, for false witnessing was one of the skills in which many of them excelled. "Oh she *did* answer to her name," they would assure us. "I was right next to her so I know. You couldn't have heard her." In that large airy park, with a nor'wester whistling through the trees, perhaps – just perhaps – they were speaking the truth. By the time we made a decision on the matter, the following sports periods would be upon us, and our attention would be diverted to the new evasions.

Checking on absentees would have been little enough hardship had there been any sign of enthusiasm among those who eventually reached the park. But few of them showed interest in the sports of our choosing. As the boys used the other end of the park on the same afternoon, some of the girls preferred to meet their male friends behind the changing sheds, for entertainment more to their taste. We had to leave the courts or the playing fields from time to time to chase a flash of blue uniform which had appeared from behind a distant tree, or the owner of a foot left carelessly poking out under a hedge.

75

We chased, because it was our duty to do so, and sometimes the offenders were so engrossed that we caught them. Usually they saw us coming, and then it was easy to escape us for in spite of their lack of training, they could still run a little faster than we could. In the meantime our basketball teams would have either sat down on the court, or would have "gone for a drink", an excursion which took some time, because they chose the farthest tap and came back slowly by the longest route they dared take. Then no one remembered the score. No one in fact was very interested in the score, but it made a useful subject for a stand-up argument which delayed their return to the game.

Once a term a form contest was held, and this roused some interest. But it was difficult to referee, as the forms decided that rules should not count in anything which really mattered – the play was the thing, no holds barred, and heaven help anyone who pushed the centre forward of *their* team. There was one lively occasion on which Myrtle of 5HB accused Yvonne of C4A, in the middle of their form basketball match, of wearing her lost gym shoes. They decided to settle this matter there and then, and in two minutes all those playing had taken sides and there was a glorious free-for-all in the middle of the court. A prefect was attempting to referee at the time. By the time the staff arrived on the scene, the battle was at an exciting stage. It was tempting to stand on the sideline and watch, but we felt obliged to intervene to prevent the premature death of some of the combatants.

One summer I allowed the softball girls in my care to elect their own captains, who then chose their teams and named them to their taste. There were the Fabian Fans, the Hot Rods, the Goon Girls, and others. This went fairly well until three of the Hot Rods were suspended from school, and several others left. The rearrangement of teams was hindered by heated disagreement of the captains, and the scheme had to be abandoned.

For most of the year, we had to contend with an apathy among the girls, which made them unwilling to move about the park even on cold days. They would sit as far away from us as they dared, until we approached and urged them, or ordered them, into joining the teams. They had every excuse for not playing – they had sore legs, sprained ankles, indigestion, plantar warts and sick headaches. Perhaps they would arrive without sports shoes. We would counter this move by ordering them to run around the boundary of a portion of the park. But in this there was a risk that they would not come back. Or often, as soon as out of earshot, they would slow down to a casual stroll, arm in arm, and try to make the round trip last the whole sports period. The staff, refereeing games, would either have to desert their teams again, who would thereupon decide that the game was over, and pack up ("But I thought it was time to go home, Mrs Bream! You went away."), or else we could ignore the strollers, which was not conducive to good discipline. There were, in addition, many genuine non-participants sitting out, as the playing courts and fields allotted to us were limited, and the woman-power even more so. We would place those not playing near those who were, and try to watch them as we supervised the games. This was good exercise for our neck and eye muscles, but had little other practical use. Group by group they would silently disappear, for destinations unknown. Control in such circumstances was almost impossible, and to add to our discomfort, the park was usually too hot, too windy, or too cold – or did we just imagine it to be so? We were not in the mood to enjoy the elements.

Rain depended for its advantage on the presence or

absence of Miss McComish. Miss McComish was built strongly, she had a firm character, and her conscience was remarkably waterproof. If it rained while Miss McComish was with us, she ignored it. We carried on regardless. But occasionally Miss McComish had duties at school, and then we welcomed the lightest shower. While it was fine, we really did our best – we strove conscientiously and unceasingly to keep our girls in the park and on the move. But at the first drop of light rain, we felt a glorious peace overwhelm us. Nature had intervened on our behalf, and it would be ungracious to spurn her gift. "You mustn't get wet, girls," we would say promptly. "Pack up quickly and hurry home." This worked quite nicely until one unusual pupil turned up at school one day and asked for work to do until bell time. After that, we were instructed to carry on in the rain, unless there was a downpour. We gave the meaning of "downpour" rather wide scope, but it was never quite the same.

The only Thursdays we welcomed were those on which it poured with rain before we left. There was then no excursion to the park. Instead we took classes – any allotted to us – in our rooms. This had an element of chance about it which appealed to both pupils and staff. There were always the lucky days on which we were given one of the few top classes, and in any case, the worst class safely seated in our room, was preferable to the chaos of the park.

The other dreaded event was duty day. There were about a hundred more boys than girls at the school, but the numbers of men and women teachers were not in the same proportion, and the women formed a very small minority. This meant that our duty day came frequently. We had one each week, while the men took duty once a fortnight, and even then they worked in twos. We resented this a little, but we knew that it was inevitable. We had to admit that the presence of a woman duty teacher was necessary, not only for sickroom duties, but because only a woman understands the devious turnings of a feminine juvenile mind, and the depths of low cunning to which the female sex can resort.

Duty began for us at eight-thirty. From then until the assembly bell, we were to see that bicycles were placed in the stands provided, and not leaned carelessly against the nearest wall, that girls moved quickly to the cloakrooms, and then to their lockers to collect their morning's books, that there was no unseemly behaviour such as hiding one another's satchel or tearing someone else's blouse or hanging one's hat on another's peg or shrieking loudly enough to disturb the office staff or holding a friend's head too long under the water tap. We were to have a brief look at uniform, and to check for rings, pendants, bracelets, lipstick, nail polish and eye shadow.

At ten to nine, a bell rang as a signal for the school to line up outside the hall in the separate classes, in order to march into assembly. A special place was marked out for each class, but the pupils maintained an ever-present hope that the duty teachers did not know which form they were in. They liked to sit with their friends, and their friends changed their identity so suddenly and so frequently that the rows were seldom the same from one day to the next. As we grew to know the girls and their forms, there was an increasing number of rearrangements to make before they filed into the hall.

During assembly, the boys sat in one half of the hall, the boy prefects and the two men duty teachers standing in a line along the wall from where they could overlook the pupils. There was a similar arrangement on the girls' side, but the girl prefects were not as tall or burly as the boys, and had less natural advantage for over-looking. I took my place among them, on my first duty day, hoping that my mere presence would be sufficient deterrent to prevent any major outbreak of crime. The prefects were already lined up when I entered, and were intent on their job. They would swiftly dart forward from time to time, to remove chewing gum, comics, photographs or rubber bands from the girls nearest them. After the ceremony these were presented to me with a list of names, but as I knew few of the names yet, or which forms contained the offenders, I could do little except throw the more valuable articles into my cupboard in the staffroom. I noticed that all the cupboards held similar treasures, so I gathered that this was the correct thing to do. I put the list of names in there too, and occasionally a girl would come to me to ask for her property back. This was sold to her for the price of two hymns, neatly written out.

On this first morning of duty, the hymn in my vicinity sounded a little unfamiliar. I moved nearer to the rows beside me.

"Unresting, unhasting, and silent as light," sang one girl, "I saw Ken on Saturday ni-yi-yi-yight."

Her neighbour replied: "Thy justice like mountains high soaring above, I thought you wasn't speaking to him any more."

I touched her elbow and they reverted to the more orthodox version. A small plump girl with green hair was now making her way clumsily out of the middle of a row. She trod on several feet, the owners of which squeaked or jumped, she knocked down one hymnbook, and eventually arrived at me.

"I feel sick," she said.

"Take her out, please," I said to the nearest girl

80

prefect.

"*You're* not sick," sneered the prefect. "You tried this on yesterday."

"Well I *do* feel sick," said the green-head. "And I've got pains in my stomach."

"Take her out," I whispered urgently. "Get her outside while they're still standing. The hymn's nearly over."

After the hymn and the Lord's Prayer, the school sat down, and supervision was easier for the prefects, so I slipped out of the open door behind me, and went in search of the green-head. She was sitting on a seat outside, arguing vigorously with the prefect about the exact state of her sickness. I was for the moment more interested in the colour of her head.

"Whatever have you done to your hair?" I asked.

She pouted but was silent.

"That's nothing," said the prefect. "You should have seen it last month. It was pink then, wasn't it Gaylene?"

Gaylene continued to say nothing, but shot a venomous look at the prefect. She did look a bit sick – or was it the reflection from her hair? I told the prefect to take her to the sickroom, and crept back to the hall. The Principal had made his dignified exit, and the First Assistant was now addressing the school. It seemed to concern some damage to a bicycle.

" . . . so in future," he continued, "no balls of any kind are to be thrown in the playground, absolutely no balls. Anyone seen throwing a ball will be severely dealt with by me."

I felt sure that Mr Good would not have made such a remarkable announcement without good cause, but I wondered just how much of the restlessness in class was due to the enforced immobility during recreational periods in the small dingy overcrowded playground, and

81

how far the general abhorrence of sport was induced by the lack of facilities for practice during lunch time, and the habit of lounging, or strolling for an hour.

During interval, I made a tour, as instructed, of the classrooms, turning out any pupils I found – there was one senior girl having a quiet smoke at the window of my own room, as she dreamily looked out on to the street – and then I supervised in the playground. Two girls were having a tussle over a comic, but I did not intervene. The lurid love comic would be torn up anyhow, if seen in class by a teacher, and they were making quite a good job of its destruction themselves. I stood near, to prevent serious damage to the clothing or person of either of the participants, but did not stop the fight. They needed exercise, and if that was the form they preferred to take it in, I had no personal objection.

During the first twenty minutes of the lunch hour, all pupils who stayed at school for lunch were to remain seated in the playground. At the end of that time a bell was rung as the signal that this period was over and they may now move about, within limits. The playground was divided by imaginary boundaries into a girls' portion and a boys' portion, no pupil being permitted to cross the frontier. The school was co-educational, but definitely not co-recreational. There must have been a good reason for this – Mr Newall did nothing without a sound reason – but the separation of the sexes fostered a disturbing interest between them in class, and mixed forms were usually more difficult than others to control or teach.

Seating in the playground was inadequate – benches had been placed along the walls but a shortage of benches, and of unbroken walls, made the arrangement a little crowded, and it is not easy to eat a meat pie when your neighbour's elbow is in your ear. In the girls' area there was very little shade, and in summer it could become unbearably hot. Some jostling usually took place for position in the few shady patches, an activity which cooled no one down. When the weather was cold, the girls sat huddled on the benches as the wind whistled around them. Sheltered seats were few. On wet days the boys had lunch in the hall, which they promptly set upon to wreck, and the girls in the gymnasium. They could not safely be left here alone, so the duty teacher had lunch with them. Wet duty days were just a little more unpleasant for the staff than fine ones, but the pupils preferred them. These conditions were not, of course, in any way the fault of the Principal, but due to the cramped area of the grounds. I compared the green fields of my sons' school, and the throng of wrestling, running, active boys I had seen there when I passed by one day.

My lunch hour duties sounded simple:

I must ensure that all girls remained seated until the bell rang.

I was to check that all were in the allotted area, and that no girl had strayed into the boys' portion of the grounds.

The playground was to be left tidy, and all lunch · papers picked up before afternoon school.

I was to look in all the Coca-Cola bottles and smell the contents for the presence of beer.

I would be "on hand" for emergencies and accidents.

I must generally supervise the girls and ensure good behaviour.

There were no emergencies that particular lunch hour, and the pupils did not seem to find anything offensive or unusual in my smelling their Coca-Cola bottles. They handed them out to me willingly, one or two of them inviting me cordially to "have a swig – go on, Mrs

83

Bream, it's real good." My beer-detection sense may not have been acute, but I noticed no suspicious odour in any of them. My chief concern was the litter of apple cores and toffee wraps which appeared all around me, and which had to be somehow cleaned up before school started. It was almost impossible to catch the offenders who threw them down. I would watch one girl carefully as she finished her lunch, or the last few bites of an apple. She would watch me too, and ostentatiously stroll over to the rubbish bin. When I turned back to where she had been sitting, there would be paper bags, orange peel and crusts of bread on and under the seat. Her companions – still unidentifiable to me – would have dispersed.

I gave up trying to prevent the litter, and turned to the problem of cleaning it up.

"Pick that up, please, and put it in the bin." I pointed to a piece of greasy paper.

"I didn't drop it."

"That doesn't matter. We can't have it lying there, can we? Pick it up."

"But I didn't drop it."

"PICK IT UP."

"Don't see why I should. I didn't put it there."

I didn't see why she should either, but having given the order I had to have it carried out.

"I know you didn't," I said and looked at her sternly. "But I've told you to pick it up, haven't I? Do as you're told, while I pick up these orange skins." It was a bad moment, but she sulkily obeyed. After that I chose the smaller, more timid girls as my victims, and felt thoroughly ashamed of myself. I asked the other women teachers how they managed.

"You can't make them pick up scraps," said Mrs Rose. "I just ignore the rubbish until five minutes before the bell, then I send someone round with a tin."

"I do most of it myself," said Miss Harris. "But the Head saw me the other day and told me I mustn't."

"Ask for volunteers," suggested Miss Burton. "You'll be surprised.

I was surprised. I tried this course, and had to admit that it was a success, if one's object were simply the cleaning of the grounds. There was no lack of volunteers, although I could not understand the attraction of picking up other pupils' dirty paper and left-over lunch.

"Do you really want to?" I would ask.

"Ooh yes, let us do it." – "No, me." – "She did it yesterday – it's my turn."

"Why do you like doing this?"

"Dunno. I just do," was the only explanation I was ever given.

Of course there was the obvious disadvantage that when garbage gatherers were openly appointed, the rest of the pupils were even more free with their disposal of scraps. The more thoughtful would try to throw bundles into the bin as it was carried about; others would deliberately aim their rubbish so that it would land just in front of the collectors. There would be smothered laughter, but it was very hard to identify the throwers. Many would simply leave their scraps by the bench on which they had been sitting, with the knowledge that some one else would have to remove them. So I gave up this method and reverted to the struggle of wills which made lunch hour duty so painful. I knew that I must not, through cowardice, continue to choose the small or meek as my victims, or accept the offer of the willing scavengers who enjoyed cleaning up. One duty day therefore I forced myself to approach a large sullen fourth-former, whom I did not teach, but knew by repute to be refractory and stubborn.

"Would you please pick up that apple core?" I asked

politely.

"No. Why should I? I didn't put it there." This was what I had expected and feared. She looked at me in utter defiance, ready to fight her cause to the end.

"I know you didn't." This was a lie. She probably had. "But someone has to pick it up. Hurry up, please."

"But I didn't PUT it there." Here was going to be trouble.

"Of course not," I lied again. "But you're the nearest, aren't you? So you will pick it up, and quickly." This was feeble, but the best I could think of.

She looked at the apple core, and then at the girls in her group.

"*She*'s nearer," she said sulkily, and pointed.

"No, you are," I replied, "by just a few inches. Look." I made a rough measurement with an exercise book I was carrying. "Bad luck. Now pick it up." To my surprise and relief, she did. After that I made a rule that the nearest to a scrap or a piece of paper was the one who must remove it, and this system, discovered purely by chance, worked very well – so well, in fact, that I used it regularly afterwards. It is unfair, but it works, and even the toughest pupils nearly always take it in good part. Of course there is a scurry as you walk around, and a pushing of friends into suitable positions; but the victim is usually selected with good humour. It does not do much to instil any desire for tidiness, or to suppress littering tendencies, but it was the best I could do for quick results, and I had to settle for it.

I had a brief respite in the staffroom for my own lunch, then returned to the playground to be on hand, and to prevent accidents and damage to property. I was to restrain the girls from dunking one another under the taps; from flooding the toilets by plugging washbasins and turning on the water or by putting their thumbs

86

over the outlet to squirt their friends with a skilfully directed stream; from climbing on the shed roof; from turning the filled rubbish bins upside down; from throwing balls; from letting the air out of bicycle tyres or removing accessories from the bicycles; from crossing into the forbidden land of the boys; from peering into the windows of the workshops at the adult trainees; from entering the school buildings; from going out the gates; from climbing, swinging on, or damaging, The Tree; from playing with the caretaker's tools; from picking the mortar out of the spaces between the bricks and from writing rude words on the cloak-room walls. With these girlish activities out of the way, there was not much left for them in the way of entertainment. I doubt whether many really enjoyed their lunch hour.

After school began the final phase of our duty. Detention was taken every afternoon (by necessity and to get through the numbers listed), and at the same time the bus pupils were supervised. These numbered over twenty, although we were in a thickly populated area. Some were rejects from distant schools, some, for undisclosed reasons of their parents, had been sent to us from outlying districts. These pupils were supposed to fill in their time until their transport left by doing preparation or homework, but as only one woman was on duty, girls' preparation had to be held in the same room as girls' detention. The largest room was chosen, yet it was still crowded, and some of the bus pupils had to be placed on benches in the corridor. Inside, organisation and control were difficult. The senior bus pupils naturally wanted to discuss their work, and it seemed unreasonable to forbid them to do so after school hours, but their talking upset the detention pupils, who were not permitted to speak. Moreover, for twenty minutes or so, girls would stroll in late, and try to find seats.

"I had a basketball practice," they would explain. "Mr King kept me." "I was looking for my books." "I had to wash the ink off my hands." At each new entry, the detention pupils would look up – anything for a diversion – and have to be reminded to continue their tasks. The latecomers would need to be retained in the room in fairness to the others a correspondingly additional time after the normal end of detention, so this dragged on until nearly five o'clock.

Some girls had been given half an hour's detention, some an hour. All names had to be checked and absentees noted, then the work collected and sorted out into the pigeonholes of the teachers concerned. The ceremony was wearying for the duty teacher, but the children did not apparently regard it as a severe punishment. The room was warm, their friends were with them, and they frequently had nothing to look forward to at home. On my first duty day I found one girl present whose name was not listed.

"You have no detention, Janice," I said. "You may go."

"No," she said cheerfully, "but I'll do one please."

"Why?"

"Well, Diane's got one and I want to wait with her to walk home together and I'm sure to get one soon, so I'll do it now and I'll have it already done for when I need it."

I had to explain that we had no lay-by system. I evicted Janice, and she was very aggrieved.

The last bus pupils left at ten past five – a pathetic little handful of bored and lonely girls. They would not bring anything to help pass the time. I tried to interest them in sport, in draughts, in drawing, in crafts, in knitting, and in reading. Reading they disliked, and the rest they decided "wasn't worth while." On the cold grey winter evenings I would watch them shuffle slowly out of the gates. I hoped that after the long bus ride a warm fire and hot meal awaited them, but I doubted if this was so. Such a dismal finish to duty day always added depression to our own physical fatigue.

Chapter 6

In the second term I decided to review my teaching progress, and was alarmed to find that there was very little to review. The typing class was improving, certainly, but in typing I did not teach. The girls practised from their manuals, and they learned without my help, their interest in the subject doing far more than I could to further their dexterity on the keys. I served as a symbol to stand in front of the blackboard and make the lesson formal. I also marked their work for them, but they could equally well have done that too for themselves.

3HTB were slowly, undeniably, advancing in their core mathematics. They could now work out the cost of covering a factory ceiling with acoustic tiles, and how much a ton of butter would fetch at £8 a hundredweight. I hoped they would find this useful. They continued to work happily, and I was pleased with them.

But my other classes, if moving at all in their studies, appeared to be slipping backwards into a state of misconception and confusion. I could notice no improvement in their work since I had begun to take them. Teaching is itself a highly skilled art which I did not possess, but the chief obstacle to progress with most of my pupils was their sturdy resistance to learning, their obstinate objection to absorbing any form of knowledge prescribed by the school curriculum. In a few more liberal subjects they unfortunately learned only too quickly, and could have given me a few pointers.

As a teacher, I had to face it, I was a flop. My ability to impart knowledge was shockingly poor. I could lead my more amenable pupils to the fount of learning, I could push their little heads in and hold them under, but they emerged each time without apparently having swallowed one drop. As for my other duties – most of them could have been carried out more cheaply and much more efficiently by a good Alsatian dog.

"Encouragement," said the Head of Science. "That's the thing. Let them see that you're pleased with their effort. Tell them it's good, whether it is or not. Praise them. They'll respond – you see if they don't. Why, I'm getting excellent chemistry books from 5B. Atkins' diagram on the Lead Chamber process is a joy. Not quite accurate, unfortunately, but neat, very neat indeed. I told him how delighted I was, and now he's doing a really pretty job on the production of nitrogen dioxide from ammonium nitrate."

"*Do* you prepare nitrogen dioxide from ammonium nitrate?" said Mr Bowron.

"Well, no," sighed the Head of Science, "but the draftsmanship is so good it would discourage him to point that out. And he won't pass School Certificate whatever he does, poor lad."

All right, I decided. Encouragement week. I shall be patient, kind, encouraging and flattering to all my pupils.

I put it into practice the next lesson, ten minutes after the class had begun their written exercises.

"Why, John," I remarked in a voice of sickly friendliness, "you haven't started yet? Oh, I see. You're

92

looking for a nice clean page. And you're drawing a fresh margin – that's what you're doing with your ruler. How helpful. You do such good work at times that I was anxious to see it."

John looked at me with the scornful astonishment of a numskull who has found someone dumber than himself.

"I don't do good work, Miss. Hate English. Can't do it. And I wasn't drawing a margin with my ruler. I was poking Thomas – he's got my set square."

"Well, get on with your work," I snarled, " and you don't do English with a set square."

I passed on. The idea was all right, no doubt. The object of it had been an unfortunate choice.

"Why, Pauline, that's a good girl. You're doing well. But we put a capital at the beginning of a sentence, don't we? No, no, dear, *that*'s the beginning. And we need a verb in it – a doing word – no, 'ice-cream' isn't a verb. And you've left out the apostrophe in 'John's' – you know what an apostrophe is – that's right, but it goes there, no, there – after the 'n', Pauline – that's right. Now what must we put at the end of each sentence? And look up the spelling of 'wonderful' – well, borrow Linda's – just make those little alterations, then go on to the next exercise. Your work is coming along nicely. Linda, why ever are you crossing all that out? No, no, I didn't mean Pauline's version was the right one – you mustn't copy what she's put."

Encouragement did not bring the results I had hoped for. Nor did bullying, persuasion, supplication or hope. I simply could not teach.

But personal relations with the pupils were improving. My School Certificate English class looked to me for commiseration, not tuition. They were discouraged now. Few of them hoped to pass their examination, for even where their English, a compulsory unit, was of pass standard, their other subjects were not well enough learned or understood to make up the required total. They were self-condemned to failure already, and one of my hardest tasks was to convince them that there was a chance of success, if they would only try. Of course, it was easier for them if they did not hope – then they had better reason not to work, and working was such a bore. Half a dozen in that form studied hard, the rest decided it was not worth while. In trying to alter this attitude, and in after-hours help to the few willing ones, I grew to know some of them fairly well, and to understand better their aims and difficulties.

As for H3C, within a month of my arrival they had adopted me as a piece of personal property. As their form teacher I was something they could complain to, appeal to, confide in, and were stuck with. A poor thing, perhaps, but their own. When something is thrust on to you, thought H3C, you have to make the most of it. This did not apply to their studies, because they never quite gave up hope of evading them. But they knew they had me for the year, and they therefore accepted me. I was beginning to know them too. They were appallingly lazy, both mentally and physically. Many were unclean, some smelt strongly in hot weather. Nearly all were untruthful and at least a quarter of them were thieves as well. Shoplifting was their speciality in this field, and one at which they showed great promise, due no doubt to assiduous practice and an earnest resolve to succeed. The form register had to be checked not only daily, but period by period as well, so that any unexplained disappearance of articles on display in the town shops could be checked against the absences of members of H3C. But they were seldom caught in the act. They were particularly fond of chemists' shops for their operations, and would sometimes return after lunch with various brands of new lipstick and eye shadow, which they compared and exchanged during classes. They favoured chemists' shops in general, and one poor chemist's in particular. He had caught one or two of them and I think it was in revenge for this that they chose his goods to steal. It also offered more of a challenge, and even H3C liked the occasional thrill of risk and adventure.

Their other recreations in school hours were chewing-gum and paper-backed love comics. Both were forbidden, which fact added to their attraction, and I hoped that their health was not affected by the lumps of gum which were so frequently and hastily swallowed as the most effective and rapid means of disposal in an emergency. If there was time, of course, when the flavour had gone, you stuck your gum under someone else's desk lid and pressed down hard. As it dried the lid stuck, and efforts to open the desk next day would provide passing enter-tainment in the class. Or you could seal together some strands of a neighbour's hair, or roll your gum into little balls to be flicked with your ruler. Or you could simply poke it between the pages of the school text book which you had with you at the time. This made opening the book quite interesting next time it was used.

Yet I liked them. Their language was atrocious, if they thought I was not listening, but when I met the parents of one of them for the first time, I wondered at their daughter's verbal restraint and comparatively good manners. They were sometimes impertinent. But it was not the studied deliberate insolence which springs from conceit or the desire to wound. Their cheekiness was the instinctive lashing out of little animals who have been hurt – a spontaneous, unreasoned form of defence that came to their aid. They stole. They wanted a thing, so they took it – what simpler? But they shared what they stole. The one with the biggest haul would divide it up among the others. They were generous with all their belongings – no one had to ask twice for paper or pen or a rubber. And above all, they had a ready sympathy for every other living thing.

They were not popular with the staff, and had the distinction of being regarded as the worst girls' form in the school. If I were not teaching them myself, and had occasion to walk down the corridor, I could be sure of seeing one or two outside a classroom, banished for the period, or else waiting at the office door of Miss Ferguson or the Principal.

"No one else likes teaching us," they told me cheerfully.

"Why don't they? I suppose it is your own fault."

"Yes," they sighed. "It is. We don't behave. And we came sixteenth in the form competition." (There were, needless to say, sixteen forms.) "And we try hard. But the teachers don't like us. People tell them things. And Mr Good took us at the beginning of the year and he said 'You're a *nice* form. I like taking you and I'm going to take you some more.' And he didn't, not ever. They told him we were just too awful."

"I'm sure that wasn't it," I told them. "Mr Good has simply been too busy. He is First Assistant, remember, and that involves a lot of work all day. And of course the teachers like you. But they won't want to teach you if you don't behave. Now why don't you try?"

"Oh we *do*." They looked at me in indignation. "We try all the time. Hard. We try like *anything*. We were *very* good the other day in art, when the film was on, and no one even noticed."

"What film?"

"Well there was this tart and she . . . . . "

"Not 'tart', Margaret," I interrupted.

"This woman and she wanted her son to paint and her

brother he said . . . . ”

"It wasn't her brother. It was her uncle."

"It was so her brother."

"Uncle."

"Brother."

"S-sh! Carry on, Margaret."

"Well, it was her brother. And he wanted this boy to go into his workshop and he was cruel to him and they had no money and this boy's mother killed herself so the boy could learn to paint."

I did not quite follow the mother's reasoning, but decided not to ask for further explanation.

"Gee, it was beaut."

"Sad but."

"And this boy became a famous painter."

"Who was he?" I asked. No one remembered. But he had done some "beaut" paintings, which had been shown in the film. And H3C had been *very* good, and no one had seen, or remarked on, their being good, which was a shame.

Poor H3C! Their bad behaviour was to them a visitation of fate, like measles, or a maggotty meat pie. Some got it, some didn't. They were sorry about it, really genuinely sorry, but after all what could they do about it? They were always being punished, and regarded this as no more than their due. They avoided punishment if they could, by lies or subterfuge or truancy. But if authority caught up with them, well that was just too bad. They held no resentment. In fact they were far more tolerant of the teaching staff than the staff were of them.

"Mr Hughes went mad in science yesterday," they would tell me. "Gee, he was angry. He went all red and wrinkly and he told Jenny she wasn't fit to live in a good communion. What did he mean?"

"Well I'm very cross with you for behaving so badly in Mr Hughes's class."

"Yes, he was real upset. We were awful. And someone ran into his car the other day and took all the paint off the front mudguard. Isn't it a shame? It wasn't his fault."

"It costs an awful lot to have it painted again," said Diane. "My uncle he scraped his gate when he was backing out and he had to have the car door painted and it cost pounds and pounds. Can we go and sit in the sun?"

"No, of course you may not," I replied.

"Mr Frieze let us yesterday."

"Yeah, but he went away to the engineering block to see Mr Farley and the Head came out and sent us all in again. Because we were rowdy and he said they could hear us in the office and couldn't get their work done because of our noise."

"And Elaine and Heather had gone off down to the shop for an ice-cream and he caught them coming back in the gate and they've got to go and see him at lunch time."

Elaine and Heather looked modestly happy as this feat was related. It wasn't often you were sent for by the Head himself.

"And poor old Susan's got to report to you just for handing a piece of paper to Sheila."

I was not deceived by this innocent description.

"What was on the paper, Susan?"

"Aw it was just a bit of paper."

"What was on it, Susan?"

A pause. Then, "Well it was a verse." I knew these verses by now – I had myself confiscated one which had been distracting my last lesson, and glimpsed it before I tore it up.

"What sort of verse?" As though I didn't know!

"Where did you get it from?"

"It was just a verse. My brother gave it me. A cobber of his at work . . . . . "

"Come and see me after the lesson, Susan."

I didn't know what I would say to her – there was little useful I could say. The verse would prove to be indecent, unamusing, and without even any metrical scansion. Susan would say "Yes, it's aaawful, isn't it?" and would smile appealingly and frankly at me. I remembered an incident of my own school days, when I had once been caught passing a note to my girl friend in the fourth form maths class. A "vulgar, absolutely disgusting little note", the teacher had called it. She had lectured me non-stop for a solid quarter of an hour after school, deploring my shocking coarseness, my ill-breeding, and my vulgarity, with such vigour and command of language that I was reduced to a shaking pulp, and remembered the occasion with shame all the rest of my school days. When she had finished with me, I was convinced that I had that day plumbed the very depths of gross obscenity. The text of my note had been: "I've managed to book us a tennis court for after school – um yum lick lick." I wondered how that very able maths teacher would have dealt with the kind of note which Susan and her friends passed around. I wondered how I would deal with Susan's note myself. But time enough for that – on with the lesson now.

"Pay attention, everyone. I want to start you off on letter-writing today. Yes, Helen, what is it?"

"I got a letter from Ireland last week."

"She did too," confirmed Lynn, as if fearing I would disbelieve. "Gee it's a pretty stamp."

"How lucky you are, Helen," I said. "That *is* nice. Now, the most important thing to remember when you write a letter . . . Yes, Julie?"

99

"Mrs Bream, your petticoat's showing just a little at the back on the left hand side."

"Thank you, Julie, I'll fix it after the lesson. Now, concerning the writing of letters . . . "

It was rather pleasant to be treated by my class as a human being, a human being complete with petticoat. That maths teacher of mine would have considered it unparalleled impertinence for us to mention such a garment. But then she was not a human being. None of our teachers were. They were creatures apart – species all of their own, quite distinct from real persons of their age, such as our parents and relatives and neighbours. We adored some of our teachers, we loathed others, we were in awe of most of them and we treated them all with at least outward deference. But they were oddities on display, museum exhibits which we regarded with critical scrutiny each lesson. Had a petticoat been showing below a skirt, we would have giggled about it secretly behind our books. We would have later passed the interesting news on to other classes, and related it at home as a major event. But no one would have told the teacher concerned – that would have been the height of audacity. On one occasion, I remembered, a young teacher who had recently arrived and was taking us for English, pulled her handkerchief from her pocket and in doing so dislodged a pill, which rolled across the floor. In the silence its progress could be heard like a train over a viaduct. We all stared at the teacher and she blushed scarlet. One of the pupils retrieved the pill after class and gave it to her brother, a chemist, to analyse. It was an iron pill, which seemed to be news of great interest to the entire school. In the pettiness of our silly little minds, we found that a most entertaining piece of information, and gossiped over it for days. Yet we all liked that young teacher very much. And we were not

100

accused of bad manners. I knew that the reaction of H3C to such an incident would have been far more natural and desirable. Any teacher who dropped a pill before H3C would have no need for embarrassment. I could just imagine the scene. They would pick it up for her and return it with expressions of sympathy and friendly interest.

"What's it for?" they would ask. "Aren't you well?" "Gee, what a shame!" "My sister she took some like that when she had shingles." "Have you got shingles?" "Do you have to take them often?" "You can get pills now in jelly stuff that are easier to take – they slither down." "My friend she works in Woolworths she had shingles and they didn't make her take pills."

Children of my own day might have been easier to control, they were doubtless harder-working and more interested in their studies. From what I remembered, they were mainly truthful and trustworthy at my school. But I decided that the grubby, lying, lazy, thieving, pornographic-minded members of H3C were in many ways much nicer little beings.

As a class, they were infuriating, frustrating, appealing and likeable. Individually, they were far from colourless.

Denise, for instance, was a short plumpish little girl with straight brown hair, a round face, and a wide smile. She was always cheerful, yet constantly being punished for some form of misbehaviour. She talked most of the time; if sitting alone, she talked to herself. And it took very little to make her burst into a merry fit of laughter. She liked everybody, and the whole class was fond of her. She was like a friendly little puppy wagging her tail with delight at a kind word. She had seven brothers and one sister, all much older than herself, and all married. This gave her a large number of nieces and nephews which she expected us all to remember by name. She also had an aunt who had married a "store boss". I did not know whether this was a grocer or a company director, but the aunt apparently lived in what Denise considered fabulous luxury, and her doings frequently figured in our lessons.

Lynn, who sat next to Denise, and talked even more than she did, was tall, thin and spotty. Her hair was black for half an inch near her scalp, then changed suddenly into a vivid, harsh yellow. It hung lankly to her shoulders in uncombed sticky strands. Lynn was sentimental and friendly. Her parents were separated and her mother had been given custody of Lynn. But Lynn preferred Dad, who lived in a town twelve miles away, and she travelled to see him whenever she could do so without her mother's knowledge. Luckily Mum went out all day every Saturday. Lynn never knew where, but she used the opportunity to see her father, saving all week for the bus fare.

Lynn's first aim was to turn fifteen and leave school, her second to leave home and live in the same town as Dad, and her third to own a dog. Lynn adored dogs. She had pictures of dogs on her exercise books, photos of dogs in her satchel, and badly drawn dogs on her desk top. One day she brought along a little china spotted dog, which she had been given by a neighbour. It had the tip of one ear missing, and some of the spots were scraped, but Lynn was very proud of it, and carried it with her everywhere. Unfortunately, she passed it to her classmates in a mathematics lesson and Mr Hughes confiscated it. More unfortunately, he broke it while carrying it with a bundle of books back to the staffroom. He threw the pieces into the nearest rubbish bin, and thought no more about it until Lynn near the end of that week asked if she might have it back. He told her he had broken it and was surprised to see her stare at him in horror and then burst into uncontrollable tears. We explained to him the value Lynn put on it, and being a kindly soul he went to town that very afternoon and bought another china dog. And being a masculine soul, he followed the masculine shopping habits, and bought the very first one he happened to be shown. It was ten inches high, had green eyes, a gloriously red shiny nose, and three black patches. It cost him seventeen and sixpence. Then a difficulty arose – how to give it to Lynn. He had intended simply to hand it over in exchange, but we protested.

"You can't do that," said Miss McComish. "She should not have had the dog at school, and if it was broken that's her own fault. You warned her, didn't you?"

"Warned her? I told her three times to put it away. I threatened her with detention, I gave her a hundred lines to do at interval, and I sat her alone at the back of the room. Then the impertinent brat still passed it – got up when I was writing on the board. That's when I took it."

"I'm absolutely sick of that girl's behaviour," said Miss Tulley. "It's getting worse and worse. And I'm not having you rewarding her for misconduct with a seventeen and sixpenny china dog."

All Lynn's teachers agreed that she was talkative, inattentive and disobedient. They also agreed that she must eventually have the dog which had been bought for her. We considered sending it to her through the post. We thought of breaking a tip of one ear off it, and scratching the paint a little, to make it look less valuable. Then we decided that the only way was to let Lynn earn it as a prize. She must win it. But the only claim Lynn could have to surpassing her fellow pupils was the speed and frequency with which she talked during lessons. For a week we watched Lynn closely. She talked, she

103

misbehaved, she forgot her books, she neglected her homework, and she was cheeky to Miss Harris. I set an essay to be written in the weekend on Dogs, hoping that Lynn, who was lazy, would copy a good one out of a magazine and could be awarded the prize. Lynn failed to do one at all. She didn't like essays, even on dogs, and didn't intend to waste any part of a weekend in writing one. She said brazenly that she hadn't had time, because she went to see Dad on Saturday and read comics on Sunday. I kept her in after school and gave her two pages of the dictionary to write out.

Mrs Donning had another idea. She told all H3C to draw a dog, and gave them each a nice piece of thick grey paper on which to draw and colour it. Lynn's dog was drawn with great inaccuracy but loving care, and we thought we had found the answer. Then Lynn and Jenny had a quarrel over a pot of red tempera, and during the ensuing scuffle both their efforts were torn, the paint spilt and the wall splashed. Lynn was sent to detention.

It was Mr Hughes himself who finally solved the problem. He walked into his room one day at the beginning of lunch hour when Lynn, under the orders of Mr Good, was tearfully rubbing from a desk with sandpaper he had provided, the inscription:

"Denise is mad. Singed Lynn. Ha ha ha."

"Ah, Lynn," said Mr Hughes, inspired. "I have wanted those desks sanded for such a long time. So you're the volunteer."

"No, sir," sniffed Lynn, "Mr Good . . . "

"Be quiet, girl!" he interrupted hastily. "Don't you dare speak while I'm talking. It was good of you to offer to do them, but see that they are all done thoroughly. *All* of them."

"It's not fair," wept Lynn. "I only . . . "

"QUIET! Make sure every one is done. If you under-
take to do a job you must see you do it properly. They
must all be finished by the end of lunch hour."

He walked out before she could protest again, and had
his lunch on a chair down the corridor. We found him
there, heard the story, and took him a cup of tea. Lynn
made several attempts to leave the room, but each time
he refused to listen to her, told her how important it was
to see a job through to the end, and sent her back to
work. Ten minutes before the end of lunch time, he
walked in. Lynn had made a feeble token scratching of
every desk. He outshouted her sobbing complaints,
thanked her for volunteering for the job, and presented
her with the china dog. Without allowing her to speak
he sent her out of the room, begrimed with wood dust
and tear streaks, ecstatically clutching the dog, and no
doubt pondering on the strange vicissitudes of fate.

Then there was Felicity, who was "not very bright".
That was a euphemism on H3C's part. Yet none of them
could have been called "bright" themselves. Felicity
was no trouble. She worked quite hard and produced
little. She was not usually at work on the subject being
taken at the time, but no teacher troubled over this. She
was quiet, she smiled gently, and the class treated her
kindly, as not being as gifted as they, and therefore in
need of constant help. None made fun of her, none took
advantage.

Colleen was a tall, large, clumsy girl, who moved,
thought, and spoke, slowly. She wore a slightly surprised
air and a permanent stoop. Like so many large girls,
she was very good-humoured and slow to take offence.
The others liked Colleen, but were slightly impatient
of her. They always seemed to be waiting for Colleen
to catch up with them. Colleen's mother had been in
a mental hospital for two years, and Colleen kept

105

hopefully telling us that she would "come home soon." The class, acting I feel from what could only have been instinctive tact and kindness, referred often to "when Colleen's mother's back again". Colleen always looked happy at this phrase, and H3C liked people to be happy.

Jenny was small, dark and sullen, inventive in her lies and not without intelligence. She had a fund of ready excuses to produce when accused of any misdemeanour, and when she eventually ran out of excuses she would sulkily kick the leg of her desk in the same spot, so that it developed quite a hollow there during the year. Jenny had no mother, and her father beat her when he was drunk, which was often. That is, he beat Jenny if Jenny were to be found. She told me she usually got out of the way, and one night she had hidden on top of the hot water cylinder for two hours. It had been very uncomfortable and very hot. One by one in her cramped position she had shed her garments, not so much to relieve the general heat and sweating, but to place them as protection between her body and the metal top, which was of a temperature sufficient to burn naked skin. Jenny had a fear of the Child Welfare Department, with the mention of which some kindly neighbours had apparently tried to threaten her father. She preferred to put up with the beatings, which were neither too frequent nor too severe.

Julie was beaten too at times, but did not take it with such resignation as Jenny. Julie was very unhappy at home. She had foster parents whom she disliked and whose own children teased and bullied her. She came to school early in the morning and left as late as she dared, roaming the streets to avoid going home. It was for arriving home late that she was usually beaten, she told me. Her uniform was good, and her cut lunches adequate, so I did not know how much of Julie's unhappiness was due to her own conduct and resentment. But the beatings were real enough – I saw the evidence only too often.

Sheryl was fat and happy. She had naturally fair hair which was greatly envied by her classmates. "It's REAL," they told me. "Gee, isn't it pretty?" It was not very pretty, but it was certainly much better than the bottle fairness which so many of them achieved. Sheryl, however, was not very proud of her naturally blonde hair. She had another preoccupation – she wanted to reduce. So every time she called out in class, I made her come out to the front and touch her toes twenty times with her legs straight. She had consented readily to do this – it "made her feel good." Then Heather read in a magazine that a good idea was to scatter a pack of playing cards on the floor and pick them up with straight legs, so Heather thoughtfully brought along an old pack for the purpose. We counted out twenty cards and kept them in a cupboard. Mr Newall walked in one day when Sheryl was at the fourteenth dip – hair dishevelled, pink faced, some cards in her hands, and the rest of the twenty scattered round her feet. He asked no questions, and I offered no explanation, but after that we dispensed with the cards. Then Sheryl suggested that she pick up rubbish from the floor after class in future instead. I closed on the offer, and the rest of the class saw that she never wanted for rubbish to pick up.

Sheila was an epileptic, as were Carolyn and Jane. In my second week at the school I asked Sheila to read. She looked at me, went rigid, then gave a scream and a heave and collapsed in a kicking heap on the floor. I was the only one at all perturbed over this. "Poor old Sheila," said the class. "She's having another fit." When it was over they helped her up, retrieved her pencils from the floor, and found the page in her book again. They were quite used to such occasions and so, before long, was

107

I. There were so many epileptics among the girls that Miss Ferguson eventually issued all the women staff with clothes pegs. The general idea was to insert a peg into the champing jaws before the patient's tongue could be bitten. This must have been an acquired art. It certainly demanded more manual dexterity than I proved to have. I tried it once, with doubtful success. I did finally get it into the girl's mouth, and after the fit was over her tongue had not been bitten, but neither was there much left of the clothes peg. I was not sure whether eating large portions of clothes peg was preferable or not to biting one's tongue, but in any case other fits were always over before I could gain access to the mouth in question.

Raewyn was the intellect of the class. The others were all very proud of Raewyn, who worked hard and usually quietly. She was cross-eyed, shy, and bit her nails. She was also older than the rest of H3C and in the third term she turned fifteen and had to leave against her will to work in a clothing factory. We knew this was going to happen and for months had done our best to prevent it, trying to persuade the parents to allow her to stay on at school. But no, Raewyn had to contribute to the family earnings, so on her fifteen birthday Raewyn wept in every lesson. We were powerless. The class was upset and unhappy all that day, and the staff unhappy, bad-tempered and angry.

Chapter 7

"We have had to make some timetable changes," said the First Assistant. "You will lose your typing class and take over the fourth form Agriculture boys for English."

"WHAT? Not 4 Ag.?"

We all knew of 4 Ag. They were the noisiest, worst behaved, least manageable and most discussed class in the entire school. H3C girls were naughty and lazy – regarded as the worst of the girls – but they could not compete with the professional malefactors of 4 Ag., who had now over a year's experience in the moral demolition of teachers. Nor were H3C capable of the subtle manoeuvres and organised sabotage of 4 Ag. H3C were bad individually; 4 Ag. were a far more formidable force, because they hunted in a pack. They went through teachers as they went through their clothes, in a few weeks reducing them to frayed, torn, crumpled wrecks. I had often listened to the men on the staff discussing the atrocities of this form, and making brave but futile resolutions and threats concerning their future subjugation. Mr Frieze, the music master, who was highly strung, had finally refused to teach them; after an argument with Mr Newall and a threat to resign, he had been relieved of them on the grounds of ill-health. I had seen strong men flinch at the mere mention of 4 Ag. I had no desire whatever to be inscribed on the list of the fallen.

"Me? 4 Ag.? Oh no!"

"You will enjoy it. There's some bright boys in that class, you know. Their I.Q. goes up to 140."

He did not add, but I happened to know, that it also started at 80, so this was no encouragement. Moreover, bad behaviour does not necessarily occur in inverse proportion to Intelligence Rating. The more capable and inventive the rebel brain, the more intricate and insidious can the assault become.

I had already taught three mixed classes, but in these the boys were in the minority. They were noisy and lazy, but not unpleasant. When I turned to write on the blackboard they would thump one another over the head with a textbook, or quietly jab the point of a compass into the arm of an unsuspecting neighbour. But this I regarded as normal, and I did not hold it against them. As long as my eyes were fixed on them they were attentive; when I was addressing the class, they were reasonably quiet; and I was satisfied with this. I had never considered them a behaviour problem.

But 4 Ag! That was big game for an incompetent, inexperienced female to tackle. I was still reeling from the shock when I went downstairs to my classroom, and as I walked along the corridor I chanced to pass the room which 4 Ag. were next to occupy. There they were, milling in a noisy rabble outside the door, waiting for the signal to invade the room, doubtless sack it, and reduce the teacher to confusion and despair. Their faces were alert; they were presumably turning over possible plans of attack for the coming period. Some were passing the time by kicking one another in the shins; a

110

couple were earnestly trying to dismantle the fire alarm. I hurried past.

All that day I could think of little except 4 Ag. There was the time they had removed all the screws from the front row desks in C11; the day when they had taken a supply of strong rubber bands (a cut-up bicycle tyre) into the library, rolled up the *National Geographic* magazines, secured them with the bands, and entered on an organised combat among themselves under pre-elected chiefs; and perhaps worst of all had been the occasion when a young relieving teacher with a simple unsullied faith in teenagers had left them alone for ten minutes in the carpentry workshop.

I did not sleep well that night, and next morning it was outside my own classroom that 4 Ag. mustered for battle. I was more than a little frightened, but I had resolved not to go under without a struggle. I must make every effort to withstand this ruthless and war-hardened opposing force. The odds were hopelessly against me, but I would at least go down fighting. Perhaps I could even make history by controlling these ruffians for a short splendid period. I determined to use every means in my feeble feminine power, every trick which my short experience at the school had taught me, to make them cower before me.

I walked towards them. They were showing no sign of cowering at the moment. They were large, hairy and muscular. Several were over six foot and nearly all were taller than I. I looked up at them and they down at me, plotting, I felt sure, enjoyable schemes for my prolonged agonising torment, and my final annihilation. But I must not show my apprehension, or the strong desire I felt to turn and run. Attack was probably my best weapon. So I took a deep breath, drew myself up to my full five foot one inch, and spoke.

"Stop this chattering at once. Line up properly in twos. You – you with the black hair – pull your socks up. Leave that light switch alone. You boys at the back turn round at once. Now come in quietly." They came.

I waited in my room, poised on my rickety bench, until all were seated. They looked at me in silence, and I began my campaign of suppression with a short but emphatic account of my superior might. I enumerated those misdemeanours which I "would not tolerate", and the various punishments which I would have no hesitation in inflicting for the slightest offence. I did not include caning on my list – there must be no suggestion that I should require any outside help.

They listened to me politely, quietly, and with what I fancied was amused interest. When I had quite finished, one put up his hand.

"Can we have pomes this period, Miss?"

I must make no concessions. Crush them from the very start – show them I was well in command and would not be intimidated. No pomes – grammar, or something equally unpleasant.

"This is not the period in which you normally have poetry," I replied. "You should know that by now. We shall follow your previous weekly timetable, and according to that you have poetry on Wednesdays. Today we shall just run over sentence construction."

"Yes, Miss."

"My name is Bream – *Mrs* Bream."

"Yes, Miss."

" 'Yes, Mrs Bream.' "

"Yes, Mrs Bream."

"Remember next time."

"Yes, Miss."

I decided to postpone the matter of this little adjustment, and I began the lesson.

Now if there is one thing at which I excel, it is in divesting English grammar and syntax of any interest which it might inherently have. In a lesson on subject and predicate I can reach an acme of dullness which I am sure is unrivalled among my colleagues. I am not taking undue credit for this – it is a natural gift. And on that day my analysis of the distinction between subordinate and coordinate clauses would have made the index of a year book appear by comparison to be bursting with fun, gaiety and excitement.

Yet 4 Ag. took it in peace. Apart from a few smothered yawns, and some which were not smothered at all, they showed no signs of distress, and were surprisingly cooperative. They copied down the repulsive diagram of little boxes which I drew for them on the board, and then they did some exercises, getting more questions correct than could have been expected from the laws of chance.

I was not deceived. Classes, even the worst classes, are often well-behaved on the first occasion with a new teacher. I knew that this was just a temporary cloaking of 4 Ag.'s true evil character, a brief respite for me while they looked me over, summed up my weaknesses, and surveyed their position in the field. They were busily devising in their depraved young minds future methods of reducing me to a nerve-wracked jibbering invalid, and, like all good campaigners, they were simply awaiting the best moment for their initial onslaught.

But the next day they were equally quiet and polite. And the next. And again the next. By the end of the week I no longer had a violent headache, twitching forehead muscles and a drum beating heavily in my chest as I heard their footsteps approaching. In a fortnight's time I began to relax. In three weeks, I found myself looking forward to my periods with them, and I

113

no longer even regretted the loss of my typing class. These boys were delightful to teach. They were animated, alert, politely argumentative, and full of ideas. Like all members of their sex, complete absence of knowledge on a subject never prevented them from holding firm and unshakeable opinions on it, and stating them with emphatic vigour. And as in all men, this was part of their charm. Even the dullest boy in the class held his own ideas upon anything we mentioned, and was ready to express himself as best he could. Class discussions were stimulating and entertaining. We covered matters ranging from the over-population problem in China to the reason for the paint flaking on the hinges of the school gate.

They never addressed me as "Mrs Bream", however. They all called me "Miss", and some wary instinct warned me to settle for this. But they did their homework for me, they were usually attentive, and no disciplinary measures were called for. Their behaviour in class was not perfect, but they almost seemed to enjoy my reprimanding one of their number for an occasional lapse. The culprit would grin happily but not offensively, often adding "Sorry, Miss."

"Amazing," said the First Assistant, as he saw them line up quietly outside my door. "Absolutely amazing. I thought I was the only one who could handle that class."

I quite agreed with him – my control was amazing. I smiled smugly and led the class in, taking care to leave my door open, too, just in case it had escaped the notice of any of Mr Good's callers down that end of the corridor, with what competent ease I subdued the worst class in the school. It's all in the way you treat them, I decided. They recognise authority and determination when they see it. Undoubtedly my strong character and my firm

114

approach were responsible for their exemplary behaviour in my room. I enjoyed listening to the men teachers in the staffroom, as they compared wounds and recounted 4 Ag.'s latest outrages. I was careful not to boast. Apart from an occasional "Oh *really*? They never do that with me", I contented myself with a superior smile and expressions of sympathy.

It was not until one day towards the end of that term that the empty puffball of my conceited self-satisfaction was reduced by one tap to a little heap of mush.

4 Ag. and I were by now on the best of terms. They worked well for me, their English was improving at a most gratifying rate, and I was indulgent to them, because I could afford to be. I gave them many privileges which I denied to my other classes. It was, of course, quite safe to do so, owing to the excellence of my command.

But one morning discord struck. It was Todhunter who started it. They were having their favourite English lesson – "pomes" – and we were about to start a new section. I never knew why the 4 Ag. boys enjoyed verse so much. At first I had chosen ballads for them, or rousing martial verse with a strong metre and obvious rhyme, which I thought might appeal. But they used to ask if we could read others which they had seen in their poetry book – modern verse, free verse, sentimental poems. They liked to discuss the meaning of obscure lines, and whether the poet was justified in sacrificing clarity to sound, and what he had in mind while he was composing the verse. They even wrote some verse themselves, and some of it was good enough to pass in a modern anthology. On this occasion I wanted to introduce the Lake poets.

"Have you heard of them?" I asked. "Who were they?"

115

To my surprise Todhunter put up his hand. I could not imagine the tall, loutish, first-fifteen Todhunter being at all interested in the English lake district, or even accidentally knowing the names of any poets associated with it.

"Yes, Keith? Can you tell me the name of one?"

"Miss, do you live at Sandy Beach?"

"Keith, that has nothing to do with the lesson."

"But do you, Miss? *Please?*" he added disarmingly.

"No, Keith, I don't. Now about the Lake poets . . . . "

"Well, I seen you there last weekend, Miss. I mean I SAW you."

This noble effort could not be disregarded.

"Why didn't you speak to me, Keith, or wave?"

"Couldn't, Miss. You was in a car."

There was one word to which 4 Ag. had been programmed by nature to respond, and this was "car". It automatically triggered off some mechanism in their interior which washed all other ideas from their consciousness and allowed them to focus their entire senses on this new concept. I recognised the fact, and knew that I must as usual allow a few minutes for a slow reconditioning back to English poetry.

Nicholson put up his hand.

"Miss, there was stock car racing at the track on Sunday and my cousin came third in an old Austin."

"The Fords did the best. They always do."

"That driver Bowman shouldn't have gone off the track . . . he had bad luck at that corner."

Fenton suddenly intervened. "Oh, Miss, there's a new film at school on car assembly. Mr Cowley showed it to his class yesterday. Can we have a film this afternoon? We come to you last period."

It had been quick this time – off cars and onto films in two minutes flat. Almost a record. I considered the

116

request. The boys were well up in their work, and there were several interesting films at the school quite suitably related to their literature studies. But I had vivid memories of the last time I had been entrusted with the school projector. The film, after running for five minutes, had shot off the reel, flung itself maliciously and accurately at my face, and then transformed into a tangled, writhing, hissing mass at my feet before I could reach the Off switch. The Head of the English Department had been rather nasty about it afterwards.

"No," I said firmly. "No film."

They were disappointed.

"Aw gee, Miss. We've worked hard. We deserve a break."

"You've had plenty of breaks in your English. You know that. You mustn't ask for too much. I've treated you boys pretty well."

Fenton gasped. There was a sudden silence in the room. They were all looking at me with something remarkably like hostility. I had not seen it in their eyes before.

Dewhurst spoke up.

"And we've treated *you* pretty well, Miss. Haven't we?" He turned and appealed to the class, and there was a general murmur of assent. "Too right we have." "We jolly well have." They looked hurt and utterly astounded. Understanding stung through me. All this quiet behaviour . . . all this unnatural cooperation . . . It was an unpleasant moment of truth.

"Listen, boys," I said quickly. "I can't work the projector myself. Yes, yes, I know you can, but you wouldn't be allowed to. I'll speak to Mr Hood. He is showing a film to his class and to some of the staff this afternoon, and I think it's in the last period. If it is, perhaps he'll let us go in with him."

He did, and we did. My boys behaved so well that

117

all the staff present commented on it, much to 4 Ag.'s delight.

I walked home from the bus that afternoon with Harold, a member of 4 Ag. who lived near me. He told me how much they had all enjoyed the film.

"You deserved it," I said humbly. "You boys were right – you *have* treated me well, and I'm grateful for it."

Then Harold confirmed what I had already guessed.

"Well, you were our only woman teacher, you see, and we'd never had one before and we decided it wouldn't really be fair to play up. Too easy, if you know what I mean. Besides, we thought it might be rather a lark to be quiet for a change, just for fun. And now it's become a sort of habit, being good when we come to your room. We really rather enjoy it. Don't worry, Miss – we make up for it plenty during the rest of the day. Of course if they ever gave us another woman teacher we couldn't keep it up. That would be too much."

"Did anyone tell you to behave for me? Mr Good or the Head?"

"Gosh, no, Miss. We wouldn't have done it if they had."

Friendly relations were restored and for the rest of the year I continued to look forward to my lessons with 4 Ag. They appeared to enjoy them, too. They had the happy knack of making the merriest of anything placed before them and even English syntax was accepted with cheerful resignation and an attempt to enliven it. I was able to include many aspects of the English syllabus which I could not attempt with other classes, even my fifth form. We had impromptu speeches, mock meetings, and organised debates, all of which they approached with enthusiasm and good-humour. We also read well-known plays with gusto and Shakespeare was given some lively interpretation that year. It was during a spirited reading of *Macbeth* that we ran foul of Mr Good.

Harvey Brampton, the largest and most muscular boy in the class, was that day taking the part of Macbeth.

"Take thy face hence," he declaimed with great pleasure to his friend Harrison. But Harrison, as the servant bearing bad news, had momentarily lost the page in his book and was not sure whether he had really spoken his final line. He fumbled with the pages.

"Get moving," said Macbeth impatiently. He was really enjoying this scene and wanted to go on with it. "Hurry up and hence, can't you, you cream faced loon."

But the servant had not yet found the place, and did not intend to be ordered around by another member of the cast.

"I'll hence when I jolly well decide to hence," he argued, as he turned over the pages.

"You'll hence right now," said Harvey. "We can't get on till you're off the stage." He opened the classroom door with one hand and placed his other vigorously on the middle portion of the servant. Then he pushed. We did not normally use the door as an exit. Those moving offstage usually drew discreetly to one side. So Harrison was taken by surprise, and off balance. At least, we think that is what did it. He said later he might have tripped over a case which was just outside the door. But something gave him surprising momentum. He staggered backwards across the corridor, fell against the unlatched door of Mr Good's office, which opened under his weight, and landed in a most appropriate position draped over the chair which was usually offered as support to offenders.

Mr Good was a reasonable man, and a good-natured one. He had a high degree of self-control and was slow

119

to anger. But he also taught senior mathematics and was at that moment completing, for display on the sixth form wall, a carefully shaded diagram of Schonhardt's solid. It was difficult to draw, and the noise from my room had been irritating him for some time. He did not want to interfere with what was obviously legitimate and useful class activity, but he found it difficult to concentrate against our boisterous reading of Act V. He was quite unprepared for a body hurtling unannounced and uninvited into his room. The table jerked, his pencil shot wildly across his paper, and the work of half an hour was ruined. This was enough to anger momentarily the best of men, and when Mr Good looked up and saw a 4 Ag. boy in a position associated with one specific daily action on his part, his next move was automatic. In a few seconds he had lifted up his cane and administered two of the best.

All this, of course, we found out much later. At the time we heard the strokes of the cane, and Harrison returned, ruefully rubbing his seat, and wearing an expression of utter astonishment. For the first time in his wicked young school career, he had been punished without justly deserving it. By this time Mr Good had composed his thoughts. Boys reported by the staff did not normally burst open his door and present their rear so conveniently for the prescribed treatment. He had perhaps acted a little hastily. He walked over to my room to find out what it was all about. When he opened my door Harrison was still standing with his mouth open, gesturing complete bewilderment to me and the class; Macbeth and the doctor had collapsed against the blackboard, clutching each other in abandoned delight; and the rest of the class and cast were helpless with laughter. They stood up for the First Assistant, as always, but they could not control their mirth. Nor, entirely, could the teacher. That is the only time I have found any amusement in the caning of a boy. Mr Good, as I said, was a kind man, and a fair-minded one. He did not apologise in so many words. But he grinned, twisted Harrison's head round to him, and said "Well what do you expect, lad, when you barge in like that and practically beg for it?" Then he asked if he might watch the next scene or two. 4 Ag. were very pleased at this. Mr Good stayed until the end of the play, and then complimented the boys on their performance – a little unorthodox, as he pointed out, but nevertheless impressive and full of feeling.

The incident would not have occurred at all had Macbeth been played by a normal boy with a normal sized push. But Harvey Brampton was the tallest and strongest member of the class. He was a good-natured, friendly boy, always willing to help, and at first I would call on him for any heavy tasks, such as shifting desks or carrying large piles of books. But I had not then realised that when Brampton was asked to do a job he did it in the shortest possible time, with the quickest and nearest means at hand, and this was usually his own exceptionally powerful muscular strength. Any damage or destruction in the process was quite immaterial to the issue. I asked him once to open a window which appeared to be stuck. He opened it all right. As the sill splintered we realised that it had been nailed down by the caretaker because the cords were broken. Another time I asked him to fit a classroom set of textbooks into a cupboard, forgetting that the cupboard was already almost full. The books must have been forced in by sheer might and will power, for a fortnight later the bottom hinge of the door gave way under the strain, and the books spilled out on the floor during class. Once I asked him to move my table; he swung it upside down with

121

one hand. Then he picked up the broken glass and I bought another light bulb. So I learned to avoid asking him to perform specific tasks, much as I appreciated his willingness to help.

He was not, however, in spite of his size, the real leader of the form. This position belonged to a boy named Brian Dewhurst. Brian was of only average height, but he was exceptionally intelligent, and had a force of personality which seemed to bear everything and everyone before it. He could sway the class to his opinion, he could persuade them to perpetrate mass manoeuvres which any single individual of them would have shrunk from even contemplating, and his decisions were apparently law among them. I pitied any teacher who might run foul of Dewhurst. Fortunately for me, he and I had many interests in common, and moreover I knew that it would have been only with Dewhurst's consent and approval, if not by his instigation, that the class had adopted the novel procedure of being good in my lessons. It was a situation which probably appealed to his lively sense of the ridiculous. His organisation of 4 Ag.'s crimes was masterly. He foresaw all difficulties and countered them with astuteness and daring. He would have had a great future as a head gangster or the organiser of a smuggling racket, but when I last heard of Dewhurst his talents had been smothered in a dull respectable career as a share milker.

There was one other teacher, I discovered, who had no complaints against 4 Ag. This was the master who took them for agriculture, and whom we seldom saw in the staffroom. 4 Ag. worked hard at agriculture training. This was their chosen trade, and they were eager to learn. We wove agriculture and farming into as much of our English studies as we could – they never seemed to tire of it.

At the end of that year 4 Ag. told me I must be sick of giving them lessons, so they would like to give me one for a change. They had obviously talked this over – another of Dewhurst's ideas, I guessed – and were eager for my reply. I accepted, and they told me they would give me a lesson on the Cow. They had already learned, to their amusement, my total ignorance of farming and farm stock. On the appointed day I sat at the back of the room, and the lesson took place. It had been very well planned. They had borrowed from their agriculture teacher an enormous wall chart which appeared to be a painting of a cow turned inside out. All its internal organs were in full view, vividly coloured, and numbered in black. This was hung on the blackboard for my benefit, and a few members of the class took turns in explaining the chart and in giving me information on the cow – the cow in health and disease, its construction, its digestion, its utility, care and maintenance. They spoke well and with obvious enthusiasm. Unknown to me, they had reserved the last ten minutes for a surprise oral test, and there was general delight when I was politely ordered up to the front of the room to answer questions put by any member of the class. Apart from a slip on the subject of milk fever, which they had described while I was momentarily inattentive, I passed the test with honour, and they were generous in their praise.

It took me only a couple of days to forget all the boys had taught me. The cow reverted in my mind to a pleasant creature which looks over fences and chews nicely with its mouth closed. I had never been really interested in its internal machinery. Yet I continued to blame 4 Ag. because they could not remember the difference between an allegory and a fable, or the constitution of an adverbial clause. And what interest could they really have in the facts which I taught? They too would sometimes remember my lessons for a day or two, and until I could find some practical relationship between adverbs and agricuture, perhaps I should ask no more.

Years later I was standing on the Wellington railway station one morning when a large pleasant constable came up to me and playfully clapped his great hand on my shoulder. "Hi, teacher!" he grinned. It was Alan Fenton, of 4 Ag. We discussed old times. "Remember the cow?" he asked. "Oh boy, did we enjoy that day!" He referred, in the course of recalling that lesson to oxytocin and alveoli and other terms which were again new to me. Although he had forsaken agriculture to join the Police Force, he still remembered his Cow. And although I no longer taught English, I'm sure I could still have told him the rhyme scheme of a Petrarchan sonnet, or cited a few examples of hypallage.

It was in a lesson with 4 Ag. on the second to last day of the year, that I satisfied what I am sure must have been the earnest wish of all my classes – I finally rocked too far on my tottering bench, and fell off it backwards. It was Brampton who saved me. He happened at the time to be sharpening a pencil in the wastepaper basket by my table. This, with Brampton, usually resulted in chips flying out everywhere within a five foot radius, and his pencil being reduced to half an inch. As I fell he quickly and casually shot out the hand which held his enormous open pocket knife, and through my great good fortune the blade happened to point towards the floor as he caught me between the shoulder blades and levered me upright. "You traitor, Brampton," remarked Dewhurst, "Why couldn't you let her drop?" But it was he who picked up the bench and the book I had dropped in my fall.

Chapter 8

H3C were outside my door.

"That line is straggly," I complained, "Come on, straighten it up, into twos quickly."

They looked at me with friendly confidence, and complete disregard of what I had just said.

"Mrs Bream," said Diane, "Doesn't Miss Burton look nice with her hair cut?"

"She looks nice with or without it cut. Now straighten up that line."

"She's pretty, isn't she?"

Shirley protested. "Not exactly pretty . . . she's nice though."

"She's a nice teacher," confirmed Heather.

"I like all the teachers," said Pamela, "except Mr Frieze."

"Aw he's all right," said Denise. "You just don't like him because he gave you detention for being cheeky."

"Well he shouldn't have taken my comic. I wasn't *reading* it."

There began an immediate discussion on the merits and failings of Mr Frieze.

"Enough of that!" I said. "Straighten that line at once." They grinned at me, and each obligingly moved six inches or so in the direction she first thought of. I gave up the attempt to arrange a neat column, and sent them into class.

The lesson, a comprehension one, followed the usual irregular zigzag path of H3C's English lessons for about a quarter of an hour, then Julie put up her hand.

"It isn't permed, is it?"

"What isn't?"

"Miss Burton's hair."

"I don't think so, Julie." I looked round the tousled heads, the spotted uniforms, uncleaned shoes, dirty collars and unwashed necks, and decided this might be a good time to introduce a matter I had been postponing for far too long – the fact that if one omits to wash for several days, one inevitably smells. Since hair had been mentioned, I could begin with hair. It was a subject which appealed to them. Seven of them intended to be hairdressers, and the interest of the whole class was quite evident from the various hues and styles which they from time to time adopted. I did not mind the tints they favoured, although the red was sometimes startling, and occasionally, through misuse or wrong proportions, had an unpleasant purple tinge. This was not as bad as the cheap brand of bleach which some of them used, and which, on contact with the chlorine in the town swimming baths, produced a bright green. But both tinting and bleaching had one advantage – they involved at least the running of a liquid over the scalp. Susan and Colleen refrained from tinting, and their hair looked as if the only water which touched it was the rain in winter and the swimming baths in summer.

"How many of you wash your hair each week?" I asked.

All hands went up. Truth never stood in the way of a response from H3C.

126

"And how many of you brush your hair every day?"
Most of them raised their hand again.

"Yes, I could tell *you* do," I said to Christine, one of the cleaner girls in the class.

"How could you tell?" asked Pamela.

"By the way it shines," I replied. "Christine looks after her hair, I can see that. She washes it regularly and brushes it, so it shines."

"Only if you use vinegar," said Lynn scathingly. "She uses vinegar."

"I do not," protested Christine.

"I bet you do so."

"Now, Lynn, put up your hand if you want to say something. You know quite well that you must not call out like that. Yes, Denise?"

"You can use egg too. My sister Anne did and she put too much on and it stuck. Gee she looked a dag. And you can get egg shampoo in a bottle."

"And rum. The Duke of Windsor uses rum."

"No, that's whisky," said Denise. "Whisky stops you going bald. My aunt she married a store boss and he rubs whisky on his bald patch and my Dad says it's wicked to waste whisky like that, specially as it's too late anyway because he's bald already." She giggled.

"Quiet, now, Denise. Listen all of you. I want each one of you to wash your hair tonight. We'll see how pretty it all looks in the morning. Yes, Lynn?"

"I bet she does so use vinegar."

On the afternoon of that same day H3C came to my room again, this time for social studies. They enjoyed their social studies, and were usually absorbed in their colouring and their diagrams, but this day there was a distraction in the back corner. Something was evidently under examination there.

"What are you girls doing at the back?" I asked.

127

"What have you there?"

"Annette's got some beaut shampoo to wash her hair tonight."

Annette held up a new unopened bottle of shampoo.

"Isn't it a pretty shape, Mrs Bream? Heather's got some too."

"No, I haven't. Not that shape. Mine's round."

"Put that bottle away, Annette." As she reluctantly lifted up her case to do so, I walked down the aisle towards her, and so timed my steps that I arrived at her desk when she opened her case. This was a little better, I thought, than demanding to search it, although the object was the same. Yes, as I suspected. There was lipstick, eye shadow, and a bottle of face lotion, all brand new and unwrapped.

"Where did you get all these from, Annette?"

"I brought them from home."

"Why?"

"To show the other kids." She looked me straight in the eye, with no sign of embarrassment or guilt, yet she knew well that I did not believe her. Nor did she expect me to.

"Why did you bring them to show the others?"

"I'm going to wash my hair tonight. Like you said."

"But we didn't mention hair until this morning, Annette, and you don't go home to lunch."

"I did today."

"Where did you get them, Annette?"

"Heather and Yvonne have got some too." I had no doubt of it. The trio usually made their raids together.

"That doesn't answer my question. Are yours here too, Heather and Yvonne?"

"Yes, Mrs Bream." They offered to show me.

"Where did you get yours from, Yvonne?"

"I brought them from home."

128

"And you, Heather?"

"Me too. We're going to wash our hair tonight. Like you said to."

"Stay behind after the lesson, all three of you."

They did not look worried, and I knew they had little cause to. What could I prove? There was no indication from which shop the bottles had come, and I knew that an admission of theft was far too much to expect. More experienced teachers than I had questioned these three about unexplained articles in their bags. I told myself that the city shopkeepers should know them by now and take better care of their articles on display. Where H3C were concerned, *caveat vendor*.

Interruptions such as this were a necessary part of H3C's lessons, but could not be held responsible for their slow progress, because concentration by them on any one subject for forty minutes would have been an unrealistic aim. But their standard of written and spoken English remained at an obstinately low level, which I felt incompetent to raise.

A few of the more mechanical exercises in their textbooks were popular. Punctuation, for example, was "neat fun." There was such a variety of little marks you could choose from to put into an undressed passage, and so many possible places to insert them.

"I'm going to put a comma *there*," I would hear Denise announce happily to her neighbour.

"Aaaw gee, I wanted to put one there," said Lynn.

Denise was good-natured. "All right, you can have the comma, and I'll put two little dots," she would say.

But I eventually taught most of them the use of the "two little dots". It was easier to understand and apply than full stops or speech marks, and their essays were soon riddled with colons. One of Diane's began thus (I have amended the spelling), "Five of us went for a picnic:

129

my mother my father my brother my friend and me and we took some drink: lemonade coke ginger ale and we took some food: sandwiches cake meat and lollies and then we drove off in the car and passed things: the church the shops the traffic man . . . "

When I insisted on full stops, they obligingly scattered them in at tasteful intervals. At the end of the year, less than half the class could write one paragraph with correct punctuation. This, I am sure, was my own fault. I sought in teachers' manuals and English textbooks for ways to convey the use of punctuation and the construction of a sentence. I tried every new method I could find. But each time I failed.

Another exercise they enjoyed was the one where they were to fill in blanks in a series of sentences from a set number of words provided below. This too was fun – you popped one in each little space until all were used up – a happy game of chance, and it was quite exciting to see afterwards if you had landed any on the right square.

But on the whole they disliked English lessons, because their English textbooks were carefully designed to provoke thought and discussion. H3C's capacity for prolonged thought on any subject was limited, and their inclination even more so. Discussion of a shallow nature could sometimes be coaxed out of them, but to achieve this I was forced to employ devious and rather deceitful methods. Because they did not enjoy English, they tried their best to divert me to other matters, and I made full use of this desire. I knew that if I said: "Today we shall have a discussion on late nights for teenagers", or "Tell me what your views are on radio advertising", I would have at the best a feeble, half-hearted response. But if I said firmly "This period we shall study indirect speech", they would seize the first opportunity to side-track me. I had only to see that the opportunity was readily available – to mention in passing perhaps the question of radio commercials, or the word "dance" and we were off to an examination of the subject. If it started to falter too soon, I could give it new life by saying "But you naughty girls have led me right off the subject – we're supposed to be doing indirect speech." They would then take delight in renewing the discussion.

Their aversion from learning was such that I also used this device to fan a passing spark of interest in any useful subject. In one English period we might deal briefly with the requisites of good diet, the properties of hydrogen, or a simple algebraic equation. I only hoped that the other teachers did the same for me, and that they managed to insert at opportune moments into their science or cooking lessons a little English grammar, spelling or vocabulary.

Unlike 4 Ag., H3C considered most verse to be "silly", and if it had no rhyme, it was "stupid" as well. They liked *My heart's in the Highlands* and *The Ballad of Lord Randal*, and they asked to read these every poetry lesson. All others left them cold.

Prose was not as "silly" as verse, but the only reading matter from which they really derived enjoyment was that in the form of comics, where the written words were reduced to a minimum, and often consisted largely of such as Whooosh, Hzzzzz or Smack! Once a week each form had a library period as part of their English course. The library was a large cool room underneath the assembly hall, and had about it an air of mystery and gloom. It was two minutes' walk from my classroom, and transporting H3C intact more than a few feet in any direction was an undertaking with a certain element of risk. They set out in twos from outside my room, walked down three corridors, across the playground, round a couple of sheds, and then they were, or should have been, outside the library. Eighteen twos, if all were present that day, made a moving column of approximately ten yards, and this was too much for me to keep in view all the time, when the route was not a straight line. Corners were advantages of which H3C were fully aware, and they hopefully cherished a belief that the library period was "different" and therefore I might not call the roll. In my first few weeks, there were rarely thirty-six pupils still with me when we reached the library. Colleen, of course, would be missing, but I was not worried over Colleen. I knew she had, as usual, just been left behind. Felicity was well looked after by the others because she was "not very bright", but Colleen, regarded as normal, had to fend for herself. Consequently she was a permanently late arrival – in work, in sport, in understanding, and in a march to the library. I knew she would turn up in good time, and would slowly explain to me that she had been lost, or had forgotten her tennis racquet. I would not ask her why she needed a tennis racquet in the library. I would just place her at an empty section to choose a book, and this often occupied her for the rest of the period.

But there were other gaps besides that left by Colleen. I dared not leave the class to look for the ones who were missing. If I sent Heather to find Susan, Heather would not come back; if I sent Julie to bring Heather, none would come back; if I sent Raewyn, who was our good pupil, Raewyn would come back after a long time, but without Julie, Heather or Susan, and Raewyn was one of the few H3C girls capable of enjoying, and profiting from, a period in the library. The fugitives did not make the mistake of taking off in groups. If Julie had slipped over to the railway station, Diane then had the sense to duck behind the engineering block. Or Jenny might have dodged silently into the caretaker's tool shed, to

132

sit and meditate among the buckets and rakes. When I eventually found ways of ensuring that all reached the library, and made it clear to them that I called the roll in this, as well as in any other lesson, they would simply wait until marked present before making their plans for escape. It did not prevent the attempts, it merely delayed them slightly. Like all good prisoners, H3C considered it a point of honour to keep trying. Jenny, for instance, would regularly look in an exaggeratedly intent manner at the books on the shelves, edging closer and closer to the door for a quick dash when my back was turned. I got wise to this, and would cruelly let her arrive at the very last section by the door before I sent her back to the other end of the room. This would anger her. She would sit at one of the tables, refuse to read, and mutter sulkily under her breath.

When not busy plotting escape, they would form in little conversational groups. A short-sighted or non-teaching architect had designed the shelves in D shaped cubicles, the rows of books on two sides backing onto rows in adjoining sections. In Fiction A–E it was impossible to see what was taking place in Non-Fiction Bio M–Z. As my footsteps approached, a group would separate and walk to the shelves; as I left they would merge together again to discuss the weekend's activities, or the new boy in 4T. We had been instructed by the Head of the English Department to leave our pupils free all the period to "browse" round the shelves, in order not to restrict their "natural interest" in looking through the books. I don't think he had met H3C. I endured it for a few weeks, then made a rule that a book must be chosen in the first fifteen minutes. The rest of the period was to be spent sitting at a table, reading. Sitting still was not an art in which H3C excelled, and the decision was received with distaste. They brought magazines to their tables, licking their fingers noisily as they flipped over the pages, looking briefly at the fashion pictures. When I forbade magazines, in an attempt to foster reading, and to save the magazines from total destruction, they searched for books which were profusely illustrated. But these were few. Some easy and delightful readers had been placed in the library. I tried to introduce these to my form, but few of the girls could read more than one page without becoming restless, and if one had smuggled in a pen, they drew their own pictures on the printed pages, or filled in the "o"s, or wrote rude messages for the next reader. Neither they nor I liked library periods, H3C's main complaint being "There's nothing to do there", and mine that there was far too much.

Social studies proceeded far more happily than English. The class knew very little about the subject, but then so did I. Even when we pooled our knowledge, it did not amount to much. I borrowed books from the school and town libraries, I poured over encyclopedias and school texts, and I asked frequent and inane questions of all the other teachers who took social studies. Miss Burton finally lent me a notebook which she had compiled, with excellent diagrams and summaries of ancient history, and I gradually acquired some element-ary knowledge to pass on. I even learned what the little green moons were supposed to represent, and four ways to catch a dinosaurus. I learned Miss Burton's notes each evening, and reproduced them in a simplified form, with her diagrams, the next day in class. This was very satisfactory. The notes I kept to a minimum, the diagrams and pictures were abundant. The class enjoyed drawing pictures, but none took their fancy quite so much as the ziggurats. They proved to have instant appeal from the moment I drew one on the blackboard, and their fascination grew. They copied my ziggurat from the board and coloured it in. Then they drew another. And another. They began designing higher and higher ziggurats, with tiers starting at the bottom of the page and reaching right to the top. Sometimes they coloured each tier a different shade, and the resultant rainbow effect was magnificent. Annette had a good idea – she turned her book sideways and drew an especially high one using the double page. The class admired it and tried to outdo it. Denise drew one with a fire escape, Hazel put a Union Jack flying from the top of hers, Heather made alternate tiers in blue and white checks, and Julie surpassed them all by drawing on hers a host of little windows with frilly curtains. They drew ziggurats at home of their own free will, and showed them to me the next morning. They were all very happy.

But at last I stemmed the flow of ziggurats, and we began ancient Greek history. Here I was on familiar ground, having studied the classics, and I found teaching easier. I made quite a good job of it, I considered. I outlined the main events of early Greece, I explained and then gave notes on prominent statesmen and philosophers, on the government of the city states and its advantages, on the influence of Greek culture on the world today. I held their attention and was pleased with my efforts, for they seemed both to understand and to take an interest in my explanations and my blackboard notes. Then I gave them a written test on ancient Greece.

"The Greek religion," Denise's paper informed me, "was a bit like ours. Then again it was a bit like itself."

"Pericles," wrote Julie, "was a fat Greek man who used to eat all the new born babies in the temples." Then she drew a ziggurat.

"Whatever could I have said to give her that idea?" I asked the First Assistant, who saw me examining the papers in the staffroom.

"You probably moved too fast," said Mr Good. "Pupils tie up words or notions which have come separately to their ears weeks apart. That lad Franklin in the sixth has some brains, yet he told me last week that George V had trouble with the barons. You must just accustom yourself to saying the same thing over and over – *repetitio mater studiorum*. And look – the spelling's not at all bad. You mustn't expect too much from that class. By the way, Miss McComish tells me that most of them have not yet paid their cooking fees. Is that right?"

"It's right. That's one request that I do make over and over. I remind them almost every day, but they still won't bring the money."

"Keep on trying. Keep at them."

I promised him that I would, and made another effort next morning.

"Cooking fees," I began. H3C looked pained. Why bring that up?

"Most of you have still not paid," I continued. "Miss McComish reminds you frequently, the Headmaster himself spoke to you about it last Wednesday, and I ask you nearly every day of the week. Now when are you going to do something about it? It's only half a crown. Hands up those who have not yet paid."

More than half put up their hand.

"That's disgraceful, isn't it?" H3C looked as if they quite agreed – it was just aaawful, and now could we change the subject please?

"Miss McComish is very worried," I continued, "and the First Assistant has asked me why you haven't yet brought your money. Don't you realise that the material you use for your cooking has to be paid for? You take home far more than two and sixpence worth of food, and what about those lovely hot dinners you have sometimes? ... " I had said it all before, many times, but they listened politely – after all, they didn't intend to do anything about it, so there was no harm in giving me a fair hearing. I chose a few individuals to attack.

"You, Heather. You promised me on Tuesday that you would bring it without fail the next day. Where is it?"

"I meant to, Mrs Bream. Honest I did. I wrote it down on the back of my hand so as I wouldn't forget and Miss Ferguson made me wash it off."

There were, as usual, no half-crowns to be collected. They had forgotten, or they hadn't any money, or their mother would not let them have it, or they had brought it and lost it, and they would bring it tomorrow, honest they would. Jenny swore she had brought hers that morning – it was in her bag and now it wasn't. Diane had brought hers last week, she assured me, but she was tossing with Helen – "just fun like" and had lost it to Helen. Helen didn't think she ought to keep it, so they settled the matter by going down to the shops and buying ice-creams for her and Helen and Julie and Annette.

I knew I was beaten again. They all promised readily and earnestly to bring their half-crowns the next day, and we began the lesson. We studied early New Zealand once a week, a subject they enjoyed, because it covered cannibal feasts, the Boyd massacres, and the fates of several missionaries, which appalled but fascinated them. Towards the end of the period I remembered that I had not yet marked the register, and as I did so I mentioned Jeannette's absence. I told the class what I had recently learned from Miss Ferguson – that Jeannette had been sent to hospital for an operation. Their faces at once showed dismay and sympathy. What sort of operation? How bad was she? When would she be back at school? I steered them back to New Zealand history, but my

137

attempts to retain their attention on this were now futile. Even the betrayal of Captain Stewart could not hold them. A hand soon went up.

"Can we write to Jeannette? In class?"

"Yes, you may, Lynn, That's a good idea. We have English next period, so you may all write to her then."

"A class letter." "No, one from each of us." "And put them all in one big envelope." "No, separately. She would like to get them all separately."

They waited eagerly for the end of the period, and did not even demand their customary "rest". It was decided by popular vote that they would write a letter each, and then give them to me to put in some punctuation "to make them look good". I was to place them all in one large envelope and post them to Jeannette that evening. They shared out their cleanest pad paper and their pens, and began to write. They were quiet and earnest, except for occasional outbursts.

"Oooh, we gotta tell her about John in the science lab on Tuesday."

"Yeah, but it was Wednesday."

"Tuesday."

"It was not Tuesday, it was Wednesday. I know because that was the day Mr Hughes caught me on the hall stage."

"Quiet!" I would intervene. "Jeannette won't really want to know which day it was."

Towards the end of the period I walked round the class collecting the letters.

"Can we send her something too?" asked Helen.

This suggestion was received with ready enthusiasm. "Ooh yes, let's." "Let's each put in something and buy her a great big bunch of flowers." "Lollies are nice." "Flowers are nicer." "Or comics." "We took my sister some scent when she was in hospital."

138

"Very well," I said. "You can send Jeannette something if you think you can remember to bring some money tomorrow. But is that in any way possible?"

"I've got some here now," said Denise. She began to rummage in her case.

"So have I."

"So have I."

Heather asked if she might go round the class collecting contributions, and in a few minutes twelve and sixpence was handed to me. None of us mentioned cooking fees. The next morning I received more donations, and we had over twenty-five shillings for Jeannette. I did not remind them of cooking fees that day, either. I just could not bring myself to do it. I knew the members of H3C were cheats, liars and thieves, and they had the dirtiest little minds in the school. But their hearts were larger than any of their crimes.

I posted their letters that night. The fact that they had specifically asked me to read them had not in any way restrained the contents. With all grammar rules thrown happily aside, they made interesting, if difficult, reading. I put in some full stops and commas, as they had wished, and censored only one – "My cousin she was your age she went to hospitle last year for an oppration too and she died." The rest I left as they were. The spelling was dreadful, the grammar unorthodox, and there were few complete sentences. But I knew that Jeannette would love them. Narration of recent crimes and adventures was interlaced with the expression of genuine good wishes for her recovery, and her quick return to school. Each one stressed how much Jeannette was missed, and how greatly they all wanted her back with them.

Jeannette came in to see me a month later. She was almost fifteen, and had been allowed to leave school. She had been delighted with the letters, the flowers

139

and the comics. I knew by this time that her operation had been serious. I also knew, and hoped she did not, that she would return to hospital for another one. She was wearing a gay blue print frock when she called, her face was smothered in white powder, her lips a blazing sticky red, her eyelids purple, her hair home-permed, and she looked, in spite of this disguise, exceedingly pretty. She was shy and well-mannered. I was keeping in some of the class when she arrived after school, and the detention broke up immediately to transform itself into a friendly social gathering. With their happy, genuine welcome, H3C were at their best, and we all conveniently forgot that they were gathered there for punishment.

The next day Colleen lumbered up to me. I had that morning turned her out of the classroom into the corridor for half a period, where she had had to do her work in the cold – it was a hard frost – to atone for throwing Julie's exercise book out of the window at a passing boy friend. She approached me without rancour – Colleen did not stock rancour in her make-up. "Mrs Bream, I nearly cried when I saw Jeannette yesterday. It was so good to see her well again." And I knew she spoke the truth.

Chapter 9

Dorothea was a pupil of 4HTB. She had flat black hair which was neatly cut into a fringe across her forehead and a shoulder length bob. Her features were regular and she was rather good-looking. Dorothea disliked me. This may not, of course, have been very unusual or at all illogical. But Dorothea also disliked Miss Ferguson extremely. This *was* unusual and at least it put me into good company. Towards all other teachers Dorothea was polite and well-spoken, in all other classrooms she behaved well, and none of the other members of staff could understand why Miss Ferguson and I spoke of her insolence, her defiance and her unruly conduct.

Dorothea adopted, as a mission in her life, the disturbance of any lesson which I happened to be taking. I tried reasoning with her. She sneered. I poured out friendliness. She snubbed me. I appealed to her school spirit. But this was a commodity which she had in very short supply. I tried to impose my will. She sullenly obeyed me most of the time, sometimes she deliberately defied me. She behaved in the same way during Miss Ferguson's lessons, and out of the classroom she committed various acts of vandalism and disobedience which she knew would enrage us both. She probably timed and arranged these so that no other teacher would catch her in the act, or suspect her after the event. She was suspended twice during the year, as the Principal knew that Miss Ferguson complained only in serious cases, but on each occasion other teachers were indignant at what they considered a grave miscarriage of justice. It could not – whatever it was – have been Dorothea's fault. Not Dorothea, such a quiet, good, retiring girl in their classes, always so earnest about her work.

One very wet cold day, during the last period of the morning, I was taking 4HTB. Dorothea asked meekly to leave the room. I gave her permission, and five minutes later she returned. Mr Good had just called me out regarding the signature on an absence note which I had questioned, and we were standing in the corridor at the time, comparing two sets of handwriting. I noticed that Dorothea was not returning from the direction of the nearest toilets, and that she was carrying a raincoat. I wondered briefly at this, but she had not been unduly long, and there were more pertinent enquiries to make of Dorothea than the reason for carrying a raincoat down a corridor in the middle of an English period. So I said nothing. Dorothea placed her coat on top of the lockers outside our door, and went into the classroom, wearing a little smile.

Twenty minutes later the bell announced the end of morning school. When the third and fourth form girls who daily went home for lunch reached the cloakroom, they found the door would not open. It had been locked and the key removed. Moreover, the high windows, which were normally open, had been fastened on the inside. It was still raining heavily and the girls had no access to their coats.

I voiced my suspicions and looked for Dorothea. But Dorothea had taken her raincoat and departed. There

142

was no duplicate key in the office, the caretaker could not be found, the woodwork master had gone home to lunch, and the carpentry shop was locked. We noticed that the old-fashioned hinges on the door were accessible, and we eventually found a screwdriver in a chalk box among the cricket pads. But the hinges were rusted, and the screws would not turn. By this time half the lunch hour had passed, and many of the pupils had decided that moisture was preferable to hunger, and had left without coats. Others had accepted offers to share a friend's lunch. There was a queue of girls at the office, seeking permission to ring parents. Lunch break was extended half an hour, the woodwork master was phoned, and returned quickly, and the door was opened without apparent damage by half past one. Many pupils, presumably wet through, did not return to school in the afternoon. Others, who normally went home to lunch, had stayed at school, and the office telephone was flooded with enquiries for missing daughters. Recriminations began. The First Assistant blamed the cleaners, who should never, never, have left that key in that door. The cleaner in question swore that this was the first occasion on which he ever had, and blamed the caretaker for not removing it. The caretaker blamed one of the science masters, whose class had damaged the wall fitting which he had taken into town that day for repair. The Principal could not understand why the office staff had not taken better care of the duplicate key. The office staff were bitter against the games coach who had borrowed it three weeks earlier to lock up valuables of a visiting team. Parents accused the school of mismanagement. There was one letter to the newspaper. But no one except Miss Ferguson listened to my unreasonable, vindictive, and entirely mistaken suspicions of Dorothea. How could it be Dorothea, such a *nice* child?

143

As for Dorothea, she denied my accusations calmly and curtly, and wore that peculiar little smile for the rest of the day.

Her behaviour grew slightly worse after this triumph.

"Dorothea," I said one day in class. "Get on with your work."

"What work?" She was obviously bored and spoiling for a fight.

"You heard me tell the class to copy down the notes I have written on the board. Copy them down, Dorothea."

"Why?" She leaned back and prepared to enjoy herself.

"I have given you these notes to help you, and I have told you to copy them down. Do so at once."

Dorothea sat unmoving, a faint smile of contempt hovering on her lips. We had had these struggles of will before. The class enjoyed them, and I knew that my control of them all rested on Dorothea's being made to obey the command. She usually did so in the end, but the mental exhaustion I suffered afterwards was debilitating. I hoped she never knew how often victory was nearly hers.

"Dorothea," I said coldly and firmly, "Take up your pen at once."

She picked it up, held it in her hand, and then sat still again. The class watched in admiration.

"And now use it."

Dorothea looked at me for ten seconds with hatred in her eyes. Then she tipped her head back, opened her mouth and discharged the contents of her fountain pen down her throat. She faced me with a triumphant smile of satisfaction, and a "What are you going to do about that?" expression. One trickle of ink moved slowly down the corner of her mouth.

144

"Who can lend Dorothea a pen?" I said coldly. Someone passed a ballpoint and I again ordered Dorothea to start work. I was rather uneasy – a nuisance though Dorothea was, I did not want her to end her days prematurely, writhing in agonising ink-filled pain. I left the class, asked Mr Bowron next door to keep an eye on them, and sought out Miss Ferguson. It was the first and last time I have ever seen on Miss Ferguson's gentle face the faintest sign of anything resembling a desire for retaliation.

"The administration of a stomach pump is, I believe, rather unpleasant," she remarked. "There may also be an extremely bitter antidote." Her hand was already on the telephone, but when she had finished speaking, the fleeting joy of sweet revenge had left her eyes. "It's no use," she told me. "They say that fountain pen ink is not at all poisonous – you can swallow a pint of it without harm, and the contents of a pen rubber are negligible. They advised me to tell the 'poor little girl' not to worry."

I walked back to the classroom, and to my surprise saw that Dorothea had refilled her own pen and had copied down my notes quite neatly.

Much of Dorothea's bad behaviour now sprang from a desire for further suspension. She had found this such a pleasant experience. Her parents both left for work before eight o'clock. Dorothea dressed in school uniform and said goodbye to them. As soon as they had left she changed her clothes, and spent a happy day round the town, visiting her working friends. She provided herself with some of her mother's housekeeping money, to buy the necessary milk shakes, sweets and comics, and took what else she fancied from the more open department stores. She had several times been to the pictures and had once been seen at the beach. But she was careful to return before four o'clock, collect the mail so that the notice of suspension would not be received by her parents, change back into uniform, and be "just home" when her mother returned about four-thirty. All this was discovered much later, when Dorothea was suspended for a third time, and had the bad luck to have her father come home sick from work one morning while she was entertaining friends with a bottle of his sherry in the living room. Dorothea left school shortly afterwards, and I heard no more of her.

It was difficult to like Dorothea. She tore up other girls' books, she emptied their cases into the rubbish bins, she cut one classmate's new bathing costume into little pieces with a pair of stolen scissors, and she poured water into the desks. She showed no sympathy to her fellows, she was malicious and unkind. Yet she appeared to have a few friends – or at least associates – and doubtless there was some happiness in her life.

Vera was a different type. There was no happiness here. She was brought into 4HTB during the second term and I was struck by her pale face and unmoving stare. I welcomed her, and suggested she sit by Josie, a friendly cheerful soul who was that day sitting alone. Vera looked at me, then at Josie, and deliberately walked to an empty desk in an unoccupied row. Shy, poor little thing, I thought, and said nothing. At interval I watched some of the girls approach her. She stared at them, answered briefly. I could not hear the conversation, but they turned away, and left Vera alone.

She remained alone. She sat by herself in the playground, and when possible she chose a single desk in the classroom. After a fortnight, she stopped working in class. She neither talked nor worked. She spent most of her lessons in my room staring at me with a face of dead

146

whiteness, and slowly picking at her handkerchief. All friendly advances on my part were repulsed. I tried talking to her, smiling at her, trying to bring her into class discussions. She would say nothing, but glare at me with smouldering eyes. The rest of the class ignored her. She behaved in a similar way in other rooms, and in time few of us attempted to make her join in the class work. I was frankly afraid of her, or of what might happen if I strove to make her carry out an order. It was better not to give any. I never approached her desk without being sure that I had both hands free, for she always appeared to me to be on the verge of an outbreak of violence. She caused no trouble in my class. She was just a potential volcano which had to be constantly watched.

The first eruption did not come in my lesson, but in the cooking room. I was at the time occupying the room next door. H3C had found means of unscrewing an outlet at the bottom of the steam heaters – well, my room was under repair and I was taking my lesson in a spare upstairs classroom next to the kitchen. Miss McComish had a month's leave of absence then, and her place was being filled by a gentle woman, skilled in her trade of demonstration baking, but not in riding broncos or capturing rogue elephants, or whatever did fit one for teaching in our school.

In the midst of my lesson with the fifth form, I heard a scream and a scuffle. Then my door opened and a girl ran in, breathless and excited. "Mrs Bensen says please drop everything and come at once."

Adrienne had annoyed Vera by accidentally bumping her with a large saucepan she was carrying. Vera had thereupon poked a fork into the side of Adrienne's neck. It had not broken the skin, because it was, like most of the forks, old and blunt, but Adrienne had nonetheless

147

objected to this sudden attack, and she and Vera were soon struggling with each other in the middle of the kitchen. Mary was a good, sensible girl, more mature than others in her class, and often rather surprised at their childish behaviour. We could always rely on Mary, and it was Mary who now tried to stop the fight. But Vera in her fury released Adrienne and turned on Mary, gripping Mary's arm in both hands and sinking her teeth deep into a fleshy portion. When I arrived her jaws were still closed on the arm, rather like the grip of a bulldog, I thought at the time. Mary was screaming and pulling, and the class was standing about, frightened and subdued. I do not know what I would have done – probably something quite inadequate – but luckily Vera released her hold before I had to take any action at all. Vera was escorted down to the Principal's office, Mary, dripping blood in a spectacular manner, to the sick room and thence to the Outpatients' Department of the Hospital, and Mrs Bensen gave one day's notice. The last time I met Mary, she showed me the lump on her arm which she will always have as a reminder of that day.

I never found out what tragic upbringing or experiences had produced in Vera her strange, unhappy attitude. She turned fifteen shortly after this episode and left the school. She may have found some satisfaction or pleasure in her job. I hope so, but that also I never knew. On her last day at school I approached her with one final attempt at reconciliation.

"I would like to say goodbye and wish you luck, Vera," I said. "What are you going to do when you leave?"

Vera looked at me coldly.

"I'm gonna mind me own bloody business," she answered.

Alice was a fifth former, a quiet studious child. She

148

was very conscientious in everything she did, and was also an exceptionally nice girl. Her reserve and her unusual taste for school work did not win her many friends, but the rest of her form respected her and did not dislike her. She was top of my English class. Her punctuation was perfect, her grammar faultless, and she learned her work so thoroughly that she could recite at the drop of a hat the complete list of Shakespeare's plays, an example of synecdoche, or the vital statistics of an adverb. Her writing was neat, her spelling good, and her work well set out. But her essays were dull in the extreme, and I marked them low. Take the one on "Birds", for instance. The choice of subject was her own, out of seven suggested. "The various species of birds," wrote Alice, "number more than three thousand, and they are classified according to their structure. These creatures are of considerable use to mankind because they consume large quantities of grubs and insects which might otherwise damage crops necessary to the economic welfare of a nation. Seafaring birds include the martin, the gull, the albatross . . . . " Glenda, who didn't know a comma from a question mark, ignored all paragraphing, and spurned the use of a dictionary, began:

"If you reelly look deep into the eyes of a little bird, you suddingly see that its mean and eveil it looks pretty and happy when it hops and flies so we think its good but even when you try to help a bird with a sore leg that cant fly there is no love in its gase it wants to use you but they are made this way i guess so they can eat grubs without caring too much . . . "

I used to beg Alice to put individuality into her essays, to state her own opinions, likes and dislikes, to express something of her own, rather attractive, personality. She would listen politely to me and promise to try. The next essay would run something like this:

"My Favourite Sport. I particularly like swimming. The styles used in swimming include breast-stroke, backstroke, side stroke, butterfly stroke, and the crawl. The breast stroke is perhaps the simplest of these, the swimmer lying horizontal on the water, moving the arms in a semi-circular motion . . . "

"But I *did* say what I liked," she would protest at my criticism.

Alice was an active member of the Junior Red Cross, and one day she told me that she intended to enter for a nation-wide essay competition sponsored by the Red Cross. The subject was "Poisons in the Home." I could just imagine how Alice's essay would run: "The numerous poisons which the average New Zealand home may contain can be classified into three groups: corrosive, acidic, alkaline. Common examples of these are . . . " There would follow detailed instructions of antidotes and first aid procedure.

I did not talk her out of attempting the essay, but I did my best to warn her against what I knew would be subsequent failure to gain any place among the prize-winners or in the "honourable mention" list. I pointed out what a large number of other schools would be entering candidates for the contest, how much more experienced some of the High School and Grammar School pupils were in writing essays, and that she must not expect to outdo them. Alice smiled gently and said yes, she knew, but she thought she would like to try. The other teachers told me I should have stopped the poor child from going to all that trouble for nothing, but I thought the experience might be valuable to her, and it was in any case her wish.

Alice did not show me her essay – I think she was a little hurt at my lack of confidence in her ability to succeed. But a few weeks after her entry had been posted the school was startled by the announcement that Alice's essay had won first place. We were all delighted, and I congratulated Alice with enthusiasm and sincerity, but I was very puzzled. She was far too honest a child to have allowed any adult to help her. The standard must have been abnormally low, I decided, or perhaps the judges were unqualified women who marked on punctuation and spelling and nice neat handwriting.

"I still have my rough copy," said Alice. "Would you care to see it?" I most certainly would. The next day Alice brought me her essay. The "rough copy" was a neatly written version the same in text as the one submitted, which had been re-written only to improve the precision of the writing and the lay-out.

"Which is the greater criminal," began the essay, "the murderer who slays a stranger in a frenzied moment of uncontrollable fear, or the parent whose persistent irresponsible laziness brings an agonising early death to his own child? Yes, weep for your lost son, mother, but weep with shame as well as grief, for yours, yours was the hand which killed him . . . "

There were three pages of vibrant, emphatic outpouring of Alice's opinions on poisons kept at home. The essay burned with feeling and sincerity. It was compelling, and convincing and alive.

"Alice," I said to her in astonishment, as I handed it back, "it's very good indeed. Why don't you write class essays in the same way? I have been trying all year to force something like this out of you."

Alice looked shy. "I do feel strongly about poisons," she said, "and I think it is important to tell people the danger about them."

"Yes, I can see that from your essay. Is there any reason for your feeling so strongly on this subject?"

Shyly, hesitantly, Alice told me the story. Her father

151

had one evening been at the next door neighbour's, having a few beers. He stayed rather late, enjoying the company and the relaxation. But at about one a.m. he thought he ought to come home. One more, they said, just one more. He hesitated, couldn't make up his mind. Then suddenly he decided that he would not. He got up, said goodnight, and came home. The next bottle they opened was weed-killer, and his two friends died.

"And I can never stop thinking," added Alice, "that it might so easily have been Dad too."

Now that I had seen how well Alice could express her feelings, I took care to set my next essay on a suitable subject. I had sounded her out beforehand, and gave the choice of several topics, on all of which Alice had apparently held firm views. I sorted hers out from the bundle to mark first. She had chosen "Cruelty to Animals" and I eagerly began to read it.

"Steps to prevent cruelty to animals are now in the hands of the Royal Society for the Prevention of Cruelty to Animals, known familiarly as the R.S.P.C.A. Branches of this society have been established in most New Zealand towns. There are some permanent officers, and others, employed in an honorary capacity, are elected yearly. These include . . . "

Gloria, known to her friends and classmates as Glaw, was a charming child and an inveterate liar. My first interest in Gloria was the result of a test in class, in which Gloria's and her neighbour's answers were strangely similar. I rarely accuse a child of cheating in case I am mistaken. But I do point out suspicious similarities, either to textbooks or to neighbours' versions. The suspected pupils usually deny the implied charge hotly, and I have to be content with ensuring in following tests that no opportunity occurs for copying. On this occasion I sent for Gloria and her friend, and with my usual distaste for the subject, showed them both their papers. Gloria cut my paraphrasing short.

"Oh that was me," she said. "I always cheat." This disarming and unexpected confession was accompanied by a sad little smile, and I found myself liking Gloria from that moment. She mingled frank truthful statements with imaginative intricate lies, and was an expert in confusing us as to which was which. I do not know whether she had ever read *Penrod*, but she told me heartbreaking tales of her drunken father, who had driven her poor mother to find solace with the man next door.

"He's not cruel," Glaw told me, "just a nuisance, and poor Mum doesn't know what to do. He spends all his wages on the booze and brings home some awful men. They drink in the kitchen and we don't like to go out there even for a glass of water. I couldn't do my homework last night because my books were out there, and I didn't dare to go for them – well, mum said I better not, just in case."

After a few weeks of sympathy with these wretched home circumstances, I happened to mention the matter to Mr Good, and found out that Gloria's father had been dead for five years, and her mother was a highly respected member of the Women's Fellowship at the church which Mr Good attended. As far as Mr Good knew, she had no romantic interest in the man next door, who was an octogenarian living with his widowed daughter and her family.

"But I went to detention for not doing my homework. I didn't use that to get out of detention," said Glaw.

"That is not the point, Gloria. You told me a pack of terrible lies."

"But I didn't *use* them," replied Gloria. "I really didn't do my homework because I couldn't be bothered,

153

and you caught me out, so I went to detention for it."

She had, too. She had arrived at the detention room and insisted that she had a detention from me, not entered in the book. She had a strange sense of honour where her lies were concerned. She would never use lies to get herself out of trouble. Accused of writing on a desk, she would confess at once, and freely show us some other desks we had overlooked, on which she had also written. If she arrived late and was caught she would be most generous in her estimate of the time she must make up. But lying to help others in trouble was a different matter. She developed a high skill in forgery over her school years, and wrote notes for her friends asking permission for them to leave school early, or excusing their absence. Her writing was sophisticated, however she varied it, and her style convincing. She must have been successful for a long time, and a great asset to her class, before we discovered this talent one Friday morning. Seven girls, all friends of Gloria, were excused by their parents from school because they had "an appointment." She was too clever to let similar excuses come from the same class, and it was only accidentally in a chat over our morning tea, that Mrs Donning, Miss Burton and I discovered that seven of our combined pupils had similar notes. We took all notes down to the office and compared them with guardians' signatures. Four were very similar – Gloria must have had access to samples – the others were quite unlike the specimen writing. Gloria confessed at once when taxed with this. The appointments were with hairdressers – there was a "do" on at one of the boy's homes. They had all been invited and of course they wanted a rinse and set or a perm or a comb-up. She had already skipped out that morning and had her own, she told us. Did we like it? She smiled and asked how many detentions she should do? Or should she report to Mr Newall? What about sanding all the desks in our rooms? That was a tiring, filthy job, and Gloria was a clean, pretty girl.

"Tell you what," she said finally, as though we were bargaining over a business deal, "I won't go to the do." This was a truly handsome offer, and would have been a genuine sacrifice, but we told her that we had no authority to interfere with her outside activities. We settled for one detention, and spending each interval for a week in picking up rubbish from the grounds. She carried this sentence out very cheerfully and bore us no ill-will.

Gloria assured us all from time to time that she was making a real effort to be less deceitful, but there was no evidence of improvement. It was impossible not to like her. When Miss Harris, who lived alone, was ill with influenza, Gloria suddenly arrived at her flat. Miss Harris felt too ill to answer the knock. Gloria gently opened the door and announced herself. Could she please have Miss Harris's permission to come in? Miss Harris had tried three times that morning to get up for a hot drink, and had been too dizzy to reach the kitchen. Gloria had brought lemons and magazines. She made Miss Harris a lemon drink and a pot of tea, cut some thin bread and butter, and tidied the room. Then she politely asked if she might be allowed to tidy up the lounge and kitchen. Miss Harris insisted afterwards that she had not realised that it was eleven o'clock on a school morning. In her feverish dazed state she thought we must have sent Gloria round in the lunch hour, and merely wondered briefly at our choice of messenger. As it happened, Gloria had not been missed, and we decided not to ask questions this time concerning her absence.

Having a high intelligence, Gloria passed her School

Certificate with very good marks, the year before I left the school. The next I heard of her was a rumour that she had also passed a boy friend's School Certificate – that she had presented herself with his admission slip and sat his two most difficult papers for him. I have never learned whether this was true, and when, several years later, I met a grown-up, beautiful Gloria, I was tempted – oh so tempted! – to ask. But I did not. I was too afraid of the responsibility which might be mine if Gloria replied, as she well might: "That's right, and I sat Joyce's Maths the next year and Bruce's biology . . ."

I am sure that Gloria is lying to this day. I know that she will always be deceitful and dishonest. But I am equally sure that she is dispensing happiness and warmth wherever she goes.

Chapter 10

I walked into my room one day after assembly to find Edith sitting on a desk, her stockinged feet pressed hard against the steam heater. She looked at me reproachfully – she had obviously not expected assembly to finish so soon, and I had no right to appear so inconveniently.

"What are you doing here, Edith? Why were you not at assembly?"

"My feet were wet."

"How could they be wet? It's not raining. It's a lovely morning."

No answer.

"You should not be here without permission. Put on your shoes quickly and go to your class."

Edith slid off the desk, and after a fumbling and a clatter she shuffled forward, trying without success to hide her left foot behind her right and her right behind successive desk legs. She was now wearing a pair of bright silvered evening shoes, which had heels two inches high, and were several sizes too large for her.

"Why?" I pointed. Edith did not answer, but looked down at her feet as if she too could not understand the presence on them of silver evening shoes.

"Where are your school shoes? Being mended?"

"No." Edith began to cry. "They're new."

"Well, where are they?"

"I lost them on the way to school. Mum'll go mad."

"How could you lose them? What happened?"

A long pause, then, "They sort of went over a fence."

"Were they too loose?" Perhaps Edith had been kicking in joy and had sent the shoes flying off. But Edith was not the joyfully kicking type. She was lazy and harmless, a chattering nuisance in class, but only too easily squashed. She would not kick off her shoes in a burst of *joie de vivre*.

"Who was with you?"

"Susan." Well, strange things often happened when Susan was around.

"Put those shoes in my cupboard, Edith, take off your stockings and go barefoot to the first class. You and Susan will come to see me at interval."

I gave her a note for her teacher – a polite request to suspend awkward enquiries – and draped her stockings over the heater. She had been telling the truth about them – their feet were quite wet.

At interval she and Susan came to the staffroom. Edith was now wearing borrowed gym shoes, but she looked even more distressed. Her eyes were red and swollen, and she would not speak. It was from Susan that I wrenched the story.

Susan and Edith had been walking to school together, Edith wearing, for the first time, a pair of brand new shoes. They were hard at the heels, and began to hurt her as they rubbed. She had nearly a mile to walk and after a while the discomfort became unbearable.

"Take them off," suggested Susan. "Perhaps we can pound the leather and soften them." Her intentions were good. Edith took off her shoes and they began examining the lining in the heels.

"Squeeze them and work them about," advised Susan. Edith gently fingered the heels. "Oh not like that! Here, give them to me," said Susan impatiently, and took them from her hands. Edith accused her of snatching, and with some unaccustomed spirit observed that they were her shoes and that she should be the one to deal with them. Susan said she was too slow. Edith said she was not. Thus simply did quarrels start among H3C girls. After a few minutes' arguing and mutual insults, Susan lost her temper and threw both shoes over the nearest fence, with an "All right then, go and get them if you want them."

Edith pointed out mildly that she had only stockings on her feet, and that it might be a gravel path, which would hurt her to walk on. Susan saw her point. Thus simply did the quarrels of H3C usually end. Susan would, therefore, go and get the shoes while Edith would stand in a patch of long grass at the side of the footpath, so that her feet could not be seen by any teacher inconsiderately passing by that way.

The fence was a high paling one, along a back garden. Susan put her hand through the hole in the gate, to open it, and was just lifting the latch when a ferocious snarling and growling started up inside. She peeped through the hole and saw a large dog, looking as if his favourite breakfast was third-form school pupils. To his right, on a trellis, was nailed a notice, now quite superfluous to Susan, "Beware of the dog." The trellis fence stretched right across the section, shutting off the front portion of the property, yet it did not occur to Susan to go to the front door and ring the bell. Edith's feet and stockings were now wet, through standing in the grass which still retained some of the previous night's frost, and she feared the consequences of appearing at school in stockinged feet. Susan had an idea. Her aunt

159

lived two streets away. Edith remained in the grass while Susan ran to her aunt's. The aunt was already out, and the house locked, but in the shed Susan had the good fortune to find a pair of shoes, evidently waiting to have the soles repaired. It was a pity they were evening shoes, but they were better than nothing. She ran back with them to Edith, who shuffled to school just in time for the bell. But she dared not appear in assembly.

Edith was again weeping while Susan told me this. Her main concern now was not the fear of being punished by me, but the loss of her new shoes, because Mum would "just go mad" if she arrived home without them. And she was due home for lunch. Fortunately they remembered the name of the street, and could describe the house, which was on a corner.

"Shall I go and get them now?" asked Susan hopefully. "I could go to the front part and ask the people to look for them."

"You should have done that this morning," I growled. "No, you may not go." Susan's one constant desire at school was to miss school, and this would bestow too great a reward for the trouble she had caused.

My timetable was full until lunchtime, but Miss Burton was free next period, and Miss Burton was a good-natured young lady who had a car. She drove at once to the house, composing possible opening sentences. "May I please collect a pair of shoes from your back yard?" "One of our pupils left her shoes in your vegetable garden." She was slightly relieved to find no one at home. She was not above trespass in such a cause, but the ferocity of the dog had not been exaggerated. She returned to school.

There was now only one more period before lunch, and Edith, we knew, had good reason to fear the results, if Mum "went mad." Mrs Donning had met Mum, and insisted that Edith, however naughty she had been, must not go home without her shoes. Three of the men were free next period and we decided to appeal to them. They were busy, they had marking to do, examination papers to prepare. They grumbled, protested, swore, and agreed. Armed with a weapon each – a hockey stick, a cricket bat and a cane – they set off down the street. We wished we had been able to witness the operation, and their advance upon the dog. They brought back the shoes with a masculine superior grunt of "Of *course* there wasn't any difficulty", but our imaginations provided us with delightful visions of Mr Hercus wielding his cricket bat and Mr Watts dancing around with the cane, while Mr Fairweather searched among the cabbages. They were obstinately reticent, and we never found out what really happened. As Mrs Donning remarked, for all we knew the owner might have been home by the time they arrived. But Edith went home to lunch with her shoes on.

"Mid-year exams next week," I reminded my form.

"Ooooooh!" said H3C and obligingly shivered. They were not at all perturbed, but they knew what was expected of them.

"We can't be put down if we don't pass, can we?" said Heather. "Because we're right at the bottom now." She grinned.

"Will any of the clever ones in C3A come down?"

"Gee I hope not. They wouldn't like us – we're too dumb."

"Will Raewyn go up to 3HTB?"

"I don't think there will be any class changes," I said, "but I want you all to work really hard and do well. Remember that your reports will be made out shortly after the examinations."

The assumed alarm on their faces suddenly became genuine. Exams didn't matter, but reports could be serious. Parents had a habit of doing unkind things when you took home a bad report, and parents were, in many cases, far more to be feared than teachers. Not Sally's, apparently.

"Mum says I can leave if I get a bad report," she said cheerfully.

"Gee, you're lucky!"

"You can't leave until you're fifteen, Sally," I reminded her, "and you're not fifteen until the end of next year. So don't try it on."

"Dad says I can't go out again on Saturday night all year if mine is bad," said Yvonne.

"Mum says she's going to come and see Mr Newall if mine isn't any good."

"Dad's going to be real mad if mine isn't better than my primary school ones."

They looked at one another. Perhaps the exams were worth thinking about after all.

"Can we have this period to do some learning for the exams?" asked Pamela.

"Yes, you may," I said to their surprise. I was interested to see what their "learning" consisted of, and how long they could concentrate on their work without prodding from me. They took out their textbooks and arranged them with ceremony in neat piles. Then they sharpened their pencils very carefully and placed them on the desk. This all took some time, and was done with enthusiasm. Then they opened a book and looked hopefully at the page, as if waiting for some unseen power to transfer the facts on it into their heads. In a few minutes Hazel began writing out some words with an earnest, intent expression, Diane took up a ruler to scratch the middle of her back, Jane started to drum a pattern on

162

the desk with her fingers, Heather picked at a mark on her gymdress. But for the whole period they made an intermittent show of studying.

A special timetable had been drawn up for the four days which were to be devoted to examinations, and teachers too began their preparation. They queued for the use of the Banda, a spiteful little creature which sat on a small table in the corner of the staffroom, drank copious quantities of white spirit, spewed blue carbon over the hands of all who touched it, and on one out of every three sheets of paper inserted in its middle, produced an almost legible reproduction of the written master copy. We would go over its efforts, reprint the doubtful figures, put in the first or last question, depending on which one it had left out, and write by hand the balance of the copies required.

Desks were carried into the gymnasium, where all fifth-formers were to sit their examinations, in an atmosphere which we hoped would give them a preview of the conditions they would meet later in their School Certificate ordeal. Other classes were to sit their tests in their own formroom, but the change of timetable necessary for this lent an air of importance to the occasion.

The fifth-formers looked unhappy. It was too early to show alarm over the School Certificate examination – by tradition, all thought of that is postponed until the third term – but the change of timetable, and the fact that they were isolated from the rest of the school, unsettled them and made them vaguely uneasy. They began doing their homework, and briefly attending in class.

H3C soon forgot all about their reports, and any connection these might have with examinations. They were slightly pleased and interested because something a little unusual was about to happen, and at times slightly depressed because their results would be so bad. It did not occur to many of them to do any study at home. If they could not do the exam paper, that would be merely an additional blow of fate, or gross unfairness on the part of the teacher who had set them questions they could not answer. In any case, it was hardly a matter in which they could interfere.

But I must not misjudge them. I noticed that some preparation really had taken place, because there were at least five new fountain pens, which I presumed to be an involuntary donation to the occasion by Woolworths Ltd.

On the first day of the examinations they were waiting for me excitedly. All sign of despondency had gone.

"It's our English exam today, isn't it?"

"Have you asked anything on pronouns, 'cause I don't know them."

"Does it matter if we spell wrong?"

"Mrs Bream, which end is the predicate?"

There was a look of happy expectancy on their faces. I sent them in and settled them down, amid the usual barrage of questions, remarks and items of totally irrelevant information.

"Raewyn will come first, won't she?" "She always does." "Mr Bowron's sister got married on Saturday." "Helen's away." "She's stayed away because of the exams." "*I* didn't – exams are beaut fun." "Aw how do you know? You haven't had any yet." "I had them at primary, didn't I? They're beaut fun." "Did you see Shirley's new hair-do, Mrs Bream?"

I had something to do before the exam started.

"Jennifer," I said, "I want you to sit in that single desk today."

"Why?" Her jaw dropped.

164

"In the last test your answers were very much the same as Margaret's. I think you had better sit separately."

Jenny assumed a look of stunned astonishment and indignation at this accusation – for a moment the monstrous suggestion deprived her of speech. Then she broke into a flood of denial.

"Oh Mrs Bream! I didn't copy – I never never copy – I wouldn't do that! Oh!" She rolled her eyes to the ceiling and panted. "Oh I didn't! True I didn't! I just wouldn't! Oh Mrs Bream! God's honour I didn't!" Then she looked at me again with the steady wide-open gaze of the truly practised liar.

"I am not saying that you did, Jenny. And unfortunately for you, it was the wrong answers which were the same, not the right ones. It's strange that you and Margaret should have made exactly the same mistakes."

I knew quite well that mousy, spineless little Margaret would not even have enough initiative to copy her neighbour's work, and I looked to her for denial of the implication. She sat, rather unhappily pink, and said nothing. Jenny turned on her a face expressive of kind forgiveness and slight contempt.

"Oh Margaret, did you copy my answers?" she asked in a tone of sad astonishment. "*Did* you?"

Margaret shook her head slightly and became red in the face – a perfect picture of embarrassed guilt. Poor Margaret would seldom defend herself. I knew she would go through life cringing under fate's misdirected blows, with not even a feeble attempt to ward them off.

I shifted Jennifer and gave out the examination papers upside down. The class was quiet and watchful. "Beaut fun", obviously. Anything for a change.

"Leave your papers upside down. Don't turn them over until I tell you to. No talking whatever from now on. You all know the examination conditions. Remember you must not use your dictionaries in this exam. So all books away. Don't touch your exam papers yet. Turn round, Pamela. Leave your case alone, Beverley. Don't touch your papers yet. Everyone got ink? Who can lend Yvonne some pad paper? Thank you, Jane. Don't touch your papers – wait till I tell you. Well, where *is* your satchel, Gail? Never mind now – Diane is going to lend you a pen. Thank you, Diane. Don't touch your papers. Remember, no dictionaries out this time – no books out at all. And no talking whatever during the exam. Now, everyone ready? Then turn your papers over."

"We have," remarked Denise.

"No talking at all," I murmured automatically. "Those books should not be on your desk, Colleen. Put them away. No dictionaries to be used this period. Leave your desk where it is, Susan. Yes, Yvonne?"

"Can we use our dictionaries?"

The exam proceeded in silence for five minutes. Tongues were out, brows were furrowed, and there was heavy breathing. All this, they thought, was the accepted behaviour, and was a courteous gesture in honour of the occasion. In actual fact they were quite relaxed and rather enjoying themselves, as they happily totted up the questions they couldn't do and the words they imagined they had never heard of.

Sally put up her hand.

"What does the first question mean?"

"It should be quite clear to you, Sally. Yes, Carolyn?"

"Is 'quickly' an adjective?"

"You mustn't ask questions like that in an examination. Yes, Beverley?"

"Have you had your hair set, Mrs Bream?"

In another five minutes, Denise gave a deep sigh of relief, put the top on her fountain pen, and announced to the class and me, "I've finished."

166

"You can't have, Denise."

"Have."

"Check it."

"Have." I looked at her work. Admittedly there was not much to check.

"But Denise, one line will not do for question three. It says 'Write a paragraph on a book you have read.' You know what a paragraph is."

"Yes, I've put it in an inch from the margin – look." She took up her ruler to prove her point. This was a relic of Denise's primary school days, when some persevering teacher had won through on the matter, and taught Denise to start each paragraph one inch from the margin. She was very meticulous about this, always measuring carefully with a ruler.

"That won't do, Denise. You must write some more about the book. Tell me about the characters in it, and what you thought of it."

"But I haven't read it."

"Then write about one you have read. Yes, Hazel, what is it?"

"There's writing on this desk."

"Hazel, there is writing on every desk. We are going to clean up all those desks before the end of the term and I shall punish anyone I see scratching or marking them. But don't worry about it now."

"But this writing is about English and it's fresh. Someone's cheating."

I walked down to see what was shocking Hazel. 'Look!" she said and pointed. Between "David loves Mary J." and "I hate old Hughes", was a column of words, "allegible illegible illegable". Obviously a senior class had used the room recently.

"That will not help any of you in this examination," I said, "and I'm sure none of our girls wrote it. Now get on with your work."

Hazel looked disappointed at her foiled attempt to produce a sensation, but all were now examining their desks. "There's writing here, too." "There's a sum here." Denise had collapsed giggling over an entry on hers, and was helplessly pointing to it as she dug Lynn in the ribs. I resolved to buy quantities of sandpaper that lunch hour.

Soon all were finishing off. This consisted of the lavish use of their red pen, and embellishments throughout each paper which hindered my marking, but which they enjoyed so much that I did not forbid it. You ruled off each answer in red, then you ringed each question number in red, and put a double red line under your name. If you had completed more than one sheet, you fastened them together at the corner by a complicated method one of them had been shown of tearing little strips and interlacing them.

Marking the examination papers was as depressing as marking usually is, when you see the results of your own teaching. My failure to pass on knowledge and to clarify difficulties was only too evident in the misinterpretations, confusion and ignorance which were clearly displayed.

4Ag's English papers were an exception to this. Their answers were, as usual, a delightful mixture of learning and invention. Marks ranged from eighty-seven per cent down.

But among the English papers of my thirty-five School Certificate pupils, five were of pass standard. The others were dull, lifeless, and immature, even in the few cases where an attempt to learn was apparent. The only highlight was the unconsciously bright answer of one girl who had been asked to use "continual" in a sentence, and wrote "Is this rain going to continual day?"

3HTB's maths were also disappointing, after their obvious progress in class. But H3C's papers were not at all disappointing, as I had expected the worst. Raewyn had worked well, and her marks were good, but little effort had been made by any of the others, and my attempts at teaching had again been a failure. Their social studies papers were at least colourful. They had not complained here of too much time, for they had employed any surplus in adding further decorations to their work. There were no ziggurats, because I had not only avoided all questions which could possibly offer an excuse for drawing a ziggurat, but had also expressly forbidden their appearance. But there were whalers' tripots, with red flames underneath, bright blue lagoons on red atolls, Mohammedan warriors, and mediaeval castles, all having only distant relationship with the questions asked. My effort to teach physical geography had met with the success it probably deserved. "Meridians," wrote Carolyn, "were people who used to chase rabbits over cliffs," while Susan explained "lunar tides" as "the water swishing back and forth on the moon as it goes round the earth." "But I knew it meant moon," she protested when I gave back the papers. "Don't I get *any*thing for it?"

The return of the papers and the announcement of marks and places was a joyful occasion to H3C. The School Certificate form had been hurt at their low results, but H3C laughed uproariously at Julie's two for English, and Hazel's four for social studies. There were only four English marks over fifty, and of these three were due to over-generosity on my part in interpretation of the answers. But none of the class was down-hearted.

"We're not very clever, are we?" asked Diane cheerfully.

"Will you raise all the marks twenty per cent?"

169

asked Julie. "Mr Hughes is going to. He promised."

"Miss Harris is going to give us another exam on Friday and tell us the questions today so we can look them up."

I gathered that other teachers were also disappointed.

The great difficulty which always followed examinations was the preparation of reports. Entering of marks and places in class was a simple mechanical job, but composing remarks to sum up in two lines the half year's work, was a demanding and time-consuming task. There is a rule in most schools that comments written on reports must be encouraging and constructive. It is a wise rule, for encouragement is far more effective than adverse criticism. Headmasters know this, and direct their teachers to express themselves accordingly. The rule is admirable, but its application calls for extensive thought and invention until, after a few years' experience, one develops a certain facility for describing a spade in various vague terms.

You do not, for instance, write "Mary is thoroughly lazy." You comment mildly "Mary must try to work a little harder." If Keith's school work is hampered by his extreme vanity and conceit, you say "Keith perhaps tends to overrate his appearance and ability, but . . . " This "but" is the important feature and must be followed by commendation of some aspect of Keith's behaviour. For the boymad truant girl who is restless in all lessons and resents discipline, you put mildly "Joan's interests do not seem to lie in school work, but it is hoped that she will apply herself with more enthusiasm next term." Beverley "shows some ability in practical work" (she baked some edible scones one day in the cookery class), Clyde "is always helpful in the classroom" (he likes cleaning the blackboard), Sheryl "never resents correction" (she's so used to it, poor child), Mary "has made

170

some progress" (you omit to state in which direction), and Bernard, that impertinent boy who calls out in class, "is always ready to take part in oral discussion". And you also, in various ways of circumlocution, state frequently the profound and undeniable fact that if a pupil worked harder his results would be better. Then you "hope for better results shortly" or you "feel confident that there will be greater cooperation next term".

I thought at first that this procedure was nothing but shameful underhand deceit, and that parents were entitled to know the truth. I wanted to write "David is cheeky", "Bruce is a pest", "Jill is wasting her own time and everyone else's." I followed directions rather resentfully, and against all inclination. But I have since realised the purpose and the wisdom of what then appeared to me to be plain dishonesty. Remarks which are correct but hurtful have little value, and usually bring only unwelcome results.

Most pupils are already well aware of their failings, even when they have no desire to correct them. Written comments which to them merely point out the obvious, are unkind and as discouraging as insulting remarks on the length of their nose or the shape of their legs. They are made to feel that their deficiencies are widely known, and assume that the teaching staff judge them on these alone. All are prejudiced against them; they'll never please; what's the use of trying? They return to school disheartened and unhappy, but not subdued. With new aggression and resentment, they determine to find their pleasures in any way which opens to them. But if you can write even "Harold prints the figure seven with exceptional neatness", Harold will develop a sense of achievement and pride. He will print sevens all over his history and his English books, and show them to his neighbours. If you don't snub him, he will extend his activities to a nine and an eight, and then to words . . . Harold has something to aim for now, and a reputation to uphold. He will be happy at school, and make progress in his studies.

Nor is there any value in adverse remarks designed for parents' eyes. There are certainly parents who do not deceive themselves, who welcome a plain truthful account of work and behaviour, with a view to guiding their child in the best way possible. To understand and help, they must know the truth. But a school report is not the place to give it. Other parents, equally well aware of their children's faults, but not so sympathetic or perceptive, will be driven by an unfavourable report to take repressive measures which breed only antagonism and secretiveness in the pupil.

And few parents are honest enough with themselves to accept unwelcome criticism of their children. They tend to reassure the child and attack the school. On one occasion a mother rang me in fury – what right had I to call her daughter "diligent"? She was never diligent at home, she never had been diligent, no other teacher had ever complained that she was diligent, she was always a very good girl . . . It was some time before she would let me interrupt.

Finding something to encourage in H3C's attitude to study was a task beyond me. I gave glowing praise to Raewyn, who deserved it, and expressed an earnest plea that she should continue her schooling. But I avoided mention of school work on the other reports. I knew that at least four members of the class would be beaten if their reports did not please, and several others would be punished far more severely than I wished. So while criticising gently their lack of application, I emphasised their friendly cheerfulness, and their willing-

172

ness to help. This I could do in all sincerity.

Unfortunately too many parents are concerned more with marks and place in class than with comments, and these I could not hide. Also, a few teachers who did not know the home circumstances of my H3C pupils had been distressingly candid in some of their subject comments. Red and blue weals on the upper thighs of teenage girls are not one of my favourite sights, so I did not carry out too meticulously the duty of ensuring that all reports were delivered. A detachable slip at the bottom, which parents were supposed to sign and return, as evidence that they had read the report, was eventually returned to me from all of H3C, but I did not check the signatures. In fact, I avoided looking at them closely. When I asked Jenny what her father had thought of her report she replied, "Oh I didn't show him *that*! I waited till he was tight and then just gave him the slip to sign." As for Julie, whose fate had worried me the most, she too returned a slip, with the name of her foster-mother on the dotted line. But I had already found Julie's report, torn into little pieces, and stuffed behind the heater.

Chapter 11

A school year is divided into three terms and five seasons. I had come in on the paper pellet season. I am sure that ever since schools were founded and paper invented, pupils have rolled little pieces of paper into balls and directed them at their classmates and their teachers by various means of propulsion. But there are variations to the sport. The pellet can be soaked in ink. This is fortunately not a common practice today, now that inkwells are no longer provided in the desks. Amusing and desirable though it may be to have an inked pellet land on the clean shirt of a friend, or better still, if one dare take the risk, on a teacher's white collar or fresh linen frock, it is difficult to dip a ball of paper into a small bottle of ink. You can gouge a hole out of your desk and make a reservoir, but this too is unsatisfactory for your pool of ink needs to be constantly renewed, owing to the absorbency of the wood. And your own books and clothes become smeared with ink, which may bring unpleasant repercussions from home and school authority. Moreover, the whole procedure is quite unnecessary, as the modern age has provided, in the form of fountain pens and other inventions, far more effective ways of spreading ink far and wide. So pellets are normally clean, and fairly harmless. Mr Pellowe's accident was an unusual one.

The most common methods of launching one's ammunition are the thumb and forefinger, which is quick and easy, but lacks power; a rubber band which gives greater distance, but which is apt to fly away itself and be lost when used by a novice; and a ruler, which is the best of the lot, giving both speed and accuracy to your missile. But 4 Ag., being inventive, devised more interesting ballistic devices. They used the springs from their ballpoint pens, and divers oddments picked up or lifted from the technical workshops, to construct ingenious little machines which gave their pellets more velocity and force than those of other forms. They could land their bullet with amazing precision upon the chosen target. I admired their skill, but I saw their machines and their mode of action only in occasional guerilla attacks throughout the year (fortunately not in my classroom). I rather regretted having been introduced to 4 Ag. too late to witness their massed effort during the season itself. It must have been impressive.

H3C, not being so talented, favoured the ruler technique. Their contribution to the sport was the use of discarded chewing gum instead of paper. When dried, this was heavy enough to be a menace; when sticky, it was a source of great irritation to teachers, cleaners, and the unlucky pupils whose clothes or belongings had been on the receiving end. If the gum, fresh from one's mouth, was not sufficiently coated with saliva, it tended to stick to the ruler instead of flying through the air. All this was most frustrating, so to avoid such restriction you spat a little puddle of saliva onto your desk, and dipped your gum into this before sending it off. It also helped if you licked your ruler. Then you refilled your puddle. H3C were widely unloved during the pellet period.

176

Pellets retained their popularity for a long time – the season was extended even into the second term. Then came conkers. Conkers are horse chestnuts, carefully treated. To be a good conker, a chestnut must be dried thoroughly, soaked in vinegar to harden, and then dried again. After this it is bored through and tied to a piece of string. This normally provides a game for two, the contestants standing face to face, swinging their strings, and each trying to break the conker of the other. It takes some skill, and is an occupation harmless and entertaining in the right hands. But the hands of our junior pupils were not the right ones. They felt an irresistible urge to swing their conker faster and faster, and then let go, whereupon it would fly through the air in any direction at great speed, a destructive and potentially lethal bullet. Some pupils tied a conker to each end of a length of string, and tried to use the resultant instrument as a bolas to catch their friends by the neck. Few necks were ever caught, as bolas throwing is an art needing great address and experience. But heads were bruised, noses made to bleed, windows broken and the First Assistant incensed beyond normal. Conkers were forbidden, which made their possession even more desirable.

But gradually, perhaps because of a dwindling of the natural supply, the conker craze died off and the water pistol season began. After that came the paper dart period. Paper darts were, of course, with us all year, but in their rightful season they were more abundant, and more varied in shape and form. Here again 4 Ag. excelled, producing some complicated and serviceable craft, often carefully weighted by various methods to give better balance and direction. They used to show me their latest creations. I admired them, but felt obliged to add "But you won't use them in class, will you?" "Oh NO!" they would reply, with exaggerated earnestness. "We wouldn't do that!" Having both played our part, we could then discuss the ingenious method of folding the paper, and they would explain simply to me the theory underlying the shape of the tail or the position of the weights. I was once more thankful to be, in their eyes, a poor female creature "not worthwhile" misbehaving for in class.

Last, most dreaded of all, came the brief but deadly fire cracker fortnight. Vigilance was no effort here, and we were helped by the many sensible and responsible senior pupils, who were themselves so well aware of the danger involved. With the concerted efforts of these pupils and the whole staff, the damage was that year reduced to a few unpleasant but trivial injuries.

The water season was a nuisance because it came in winter. As a midsummer sport it would have been more bearable, but on a cold frosty morning, a plastic bottle of water discharged down a girl's neck was a health hazard, and puddles found in a desk or a case, which could not dry out thoroughly in the inadequately heated rooms, would sometimes anger the victim to such an extent that retaliation might take the form of a bucket full of water thrown over another pupil – the suspected culprit but not always the right one. What began as a simple fashion for carrying water pistols, developed into a glorious water festival, its object being to make as many persons as possible, and as wide an area as possible, as wet as could by any means be arranged. Water pistols were forbidden, plastic bottles were forbidden, paper bags filled with water and tied at the top were forbidden, the spreading of water by any method was punished. The Headmaster and the First Assistant spoke severely in assembly; the caning queue outside Mr Good's door doubled; the caretaker kept his tool shed locked; we made snap raids on cases and lockers; and we were instructed to watch all our classes with extra attention for the first movement which suggested reaching for a pistol or filled container. In our worst classes we dared not even turn to write on the blackboard.

H3C were in the thick of it all, and in particular disgrace. They possessed what seemed to be an unlimited supply of water pistols. I suppose it was actually limited to the extent of Woolworth's and McKenzie's stock, but these firms kept replenishing their counter boxes as the contents disappeared, so that H3C were never completely unarmed. They revelled in the water season. All the enthusiasm they spared from their school work was unloosed for the purpose. Exercise books were soaked, hymn books a sodden mass, desks and chairs wet, floors left with puddles, and the corridors they walked along were often muddier than the grounds. When H3C did finally bring their hidden energy to bear on something, they did not inconvenience themselves by any form of self-restraint.

"Beverley," I said quickly one day, "I'm watching you!"

Beverley had lowered one hand, and Beverley, I knew, was quick on the draw. She opened her eyes a little wider and assumed a hurt, puzzled expression.

"I'm only going to my case, Mrs Bream, to get another pen."

"Then open your case." There was no other pen in it, at which Beverley expressed great surprise, but I removed a Lux Liquid bottle, and a water pistol. I added these to the large collection in my double cupboard at the blackboard end of the room. The class watched the procedure.

"You ought to lock that cupboard, Mrs Bream," remarked Lynn. "We might just come in and get them."

Interfering with a teacher's cupboard was a major

offence, and one of the few which had not yet been committed by H3C. But now that the suggestion had been voiced, I knew it would find favourable reception in their minds, and my cupboard would no longer be inviolate.

"An excellent idea, Lynn," I said. "Of course, I know that none of *you* would ever touch my cupboard," (wouldn't they just!) "but someone from another form might happen to do so. Yes, I would like to lock that cupboard. But I can't. There is no lock fitted."

"You could put a padlock on," said Julie.

"Or a bolt."

"Or nail it up."

"Or put boards across."

They were always ready to offer suggestions for their own circumvention and control.

"There is no provision for a padlock either," I told them, "so I shall just have to trust you. Surely no one would do such a dreadful thing as to go to my cupboard without permission."

I resumed the lesson, and thought no more of this conversation until two days later when I went into my room after lunch. The desks were displaced in the front of the room, and there was a pile of wooddust and chips on the floor by my cupboard. A large hole had been bored – or rather, broken – through each door of the double cupboard, and a portion of chain inserted, the ends of which were secured together by a padlock. The plywood portion of the doors had been chosen for the operation, and had not stood the strain very well, for from each hole radiated ugly cracks and splits. A padlock key was on my table. While I was still regarding the damage, the bell rang for afternoon school and I heard H3C noisily approaching my door. They were obviously more excited than usual. I brought them into

180

the room, wondering whatever to say to them, but they started first.

"Do you like your lock?"

"Isn't it beaut?"

"Were you surprised?"

"We can't get our pistols out now, can we?"

Each of the questioners looked like a wayward mongrel pet, waiting to be praised and patted for bringing in all the neighbours' newspapers.

"Sit down and be quiet," I ordered. "Now it was very kind of you to want to help me, but you MUST NOT touch school property . . . Whatever will the Headmaster say? . . . nice and thoughtful . . . very very naughty . . . never, never . . . "

I talked for some time, trying to encourage their one admirable quality – their kindness towards others – and yet prevent a recurrence of this particular manner of showing it.

"But you do like it, don't you?" asked Denise a little wistfully when I had finished.

I avoided a direct answer.

"What did you do it with?" I asked instead.

"One of those big twisty things. Diane knew what to get because her father . . . "

"And Heather brought the padlock."

"There's only one key," Heather explained, "so I can't use it for my locker." All the girls in the school were required to buy padlocks for their lockers, to protect their property from one another's hands, but duplicate keys were demanded and kept on numbered hooks in Miss Ferguson's office.

"The key's on the table," Heather added.

"Do you like it?"

"Now we won't be able to take our water pistols back, will we?"

"What twisty thing?" I asked. (Had they started operations on the hardware shops now?)

"You know. Those big twisty things you make holes with. Diane knew because her father . . . "

"I've still got it," said Diane. "It's on top of the lockers outside."

"Go and get it."

Diane returned with a large brace and bit. It was a one inch bit, which had apparently been already fastened in the brace when they found it, and explained the size of the holes.

"Whose is it?" There was a pause.

"We're giving it back today."

"Giving it back to whom? Where did you get it from?"

"We borrowed it."

"From whom?"

There was a pause. "From Mr Fairweather," said Julie.

"Did Mr Fairweather lend you that?"

"We're going to take it back tomorrow lunchtime."

"Did Mr Fairweather lend it to you?" I repeated. I could not imagine Mr Fairweather putting a tool of any description into the destructive hands of H3C. "Did you tell him I wanted it?" He had occasionally lent me a tool.

"We didn't think of that," said Denise. They looked at one another – what a lost opportunity! I could see them recording it for use on a future occasion, and was sorry I had given them the idea.

"Did Mr Fairweather lend it to you?" I persisted.

"Well, we sort of borrowed it."

"When?"

"Lunch time yesterday." I knew Mr Fairweather always went home for lunch.

"Oh – you *are* naughty. You know you are not allowed to go into the woodwork shop, and you must never *never* take anything without asking. Hadn't Mr Fairweather locked up?"

They looked a little embarrassed, and gradually I learned the story. Mr Fairweather had not forgotten to lock his door. But Beverley had kept watch, Elaine and Julie had helped Annette to climb up to a high open window, because Annette was small and active, Annette had reached down and released the catch of a larger window below, then Diane had got through the lower one, because Diane knew just what to look for because her father . . .

"You will have to be punished," I said. "Firstly, for entering the woodwork shop without permission, secondly for taking something which did not belong to you, and thirdly for damaging – all right, all right, for *altering*, school property."

"What'll we do?" asked Denise cheerfully. "Shall we stay in tonight? It's a dag, though, isn't it? You like it, don't you?"

The girls concerned – about nine of them altogether – duly carried out their punishment quite impenitently, but my main concern was to hide their apparent vandalism from the eyes of the Headmaster and the First Assistant. Neither taught H3C, and therefore knew only their reputed unruliness and misbehaviour. It would have been difficult to convince them of H3C's genuinely good motive. I removed all the wood chips, wrapping them up in paper and taking them right off the premises. I did a little carving with a sharp pocketknife to round off the holes made by an inexpertedly wielded bit. It still looked dreadful. I considered hanging up a calendar wide enough to cover the damage, but a calendar over the middle opening of a double door would have looked suspicious in itself, besides being rather inconvenient.

I need not have worried so much. The following week

I met the caretaker in the corridor. He stopped me. "You're room nine, aren't you? Why ever didn't you tell me you wanted a lock on your cupboard? Gosh, you women! You take the cake. I never know what you'll do next. You fair made a muck of it, didn't you?"

The lock made little difference to the number of water pistols. With the passing of time the urge diminished, and the season closed, but by the end of it the patience and benevolence of the staff had also been sadly diluted.

"Mr Frieze was real cross with us today," announced H3C. "He bashed his ruler on the table and said 'have some sense, can't you, you silly little rabbits.' Gee it was funny. He got real mad."

The response of pupils to teachers who bang a ruler on the table and shout 'Have some sense!' varies rather according to the individual. Now Susan expected it. Compared with what she heard at home it was a nice friendly little conversational opening. She was apt to reply with a brilliant smile "I haven't brought my books" – a statement which was usually true, and which, to Susan, explained away almost anything. Joanne, on the other hand, would turn away her head and open her mouth, where it would hang, forgotten, for several minutes – or until a neighbour found a use for it by passing her a piece of chewing gum.

"It is certainly *not* funny," I scolded. "Bad behaviour on your part is never funny, and I do not blame Mr Frieze for being angry."

They waited politely and rather restlessly for me to finish. This was the usual procedure. No one listened once they realised the gist of what I was saying. But they recognised that this was part of my job, that they deserved every word of it, and that it would soon be over if they just waited quietly and thought about something else to pass away the time.

"And Jenny's not here," they continued when I stopped. "Miss McComish is keeping her all day in the fitting room. Isn't it awful? Just because she didn't have two and six for her cooking fee. It's not fair. Poor old Jenny."

"There must be more to it than that," I said. "Jenny is not the only one who has failed to bring her cooking fee. Here we are nearly at the end of the term, and many of you have still not paid. You should all be locked up in fitting rooms all day. Jenny must have answered Miss McComish back."

"Oh she did NOT," they replied indignantly.

"Then what did she do? I'm sure Miss McComish would not single Jenny out for not having her two and sixpence with her."

"Well . . . "

"Well?"

"Well, she spat in the sink."

"Whatever for?"

"Well Miss McComish said where's your cooking fee you naughty little girl and Jenny said she hadn't brought it and Miss McComish said she had a good mind not to let Jenny cook, so Jenny spat in the sink." They related this as a natural, logical response for Jenny to make. "And Miss McComish said 'That'll cost you more than two and six now my girl'. And she's put Jenny in the fitting room for all day. She said to tell you."

"It was a very dirty thing to do," I told them. "I'm surprised at Jenny." I wasn't, of course. Nothing Jenny did could ever surprise me now. I had known Jenny for six months.

"Poor old Jenny," said Carolyn. "It's not fair, is it Mrs Bream?"

"Jenny did something which was very dirty and rude," I replied. "Of course she must be punished. And have

185

you forgotten, Carolyn, that every time you say 'It's not fair' to me, you have to write out a page of the dictionary?"

At this point there was a brief knock at the door and the First Assistant entered. He turned his back on the class and spoke quietly.

"Mrs Rose says she can't carry on," he told me. "I've asked one of the men to take over her class, but I wonder if you would go upstairs and see if she's all right. She looked pretty white. I'll keep an eye on these people."

He wandered out and I turned back to the class.

"Mrs Rose is not well," I explained – quite unnecessarily, as all had been listening, and those who had heard had quickly passed on the news to those who had not. "I'm going to see how she is. Carry on with the exercises on page a hundred and forty-six."

Julie's hand went up.

"Is she having a baby?"

"Of course she is," said Heather. "It's morning sickness, isn't it, Mrs Bream? That's awful, my mother says. You feel just awful."

"Don't call out like that, Heather," I said weakly. "Yes, what is it, Shirley?"

"Mrs Bream, my sister-in-law had awful morning sickness last time and the doctor gave her some new tablets just out and they stopped it. Mrs Rose ought to get some."

"She looked pale as anything in detention yesterday," said Lynn.

"Yeah, she sat down all the time. And when Diane threw an apple core across the room she didn't say a thing."

"She didn't see me."

"She did so. I saw her watching."

"My aunt – the one that married a store boss," said

186

Denise, "she wasn't sick at all last time because she stayed in bed all morning because she can afford a maid to do her work. Gee she's lucky. If Mrs Rose could stay in bed all morning . . . "

"Stop this talking and open your books," I said. "Page a hundred and forty-six. Now work quietly while I'm away."

I found Mrs Rose in the cloakroom, white and shaking. I rang a taxi, then walked down with her to the foyer. As the taxi arrived, she turned to me and leaned forward confidentially.

"I'll have to leave soon," she said in a low voice. "Don't tell the others, but it's morning sickness. The Head knows, but I haven't told anyone else, because it would be just terrible if the children found out."

"Don't worry," I assured her. "I shan't tell a soul."

Mr Good came out of his door as I walked back to my classroom.

"What have you got in there?" he asked crossly. "A pack of raving lunatics? Can't they behave when you're out of the room? I had a parent in my office, and they were making a dreadful din. Heaven knows what he thinks of the discipline in this school. I've been in now and quietened them down, but you might have a word with them."

I promised I would, and walked in. They were fairly subdued after Mr Good's invasion, but none had worked, except Carolyn, who had used the time to scrawl out her page of the dictionary – the popular first page, which was always chosen because it was far shorter than the others. This was now on my table.

"I hear you behaved disgracefully while I was out of the room," I began.

"How is she?" asked the class, ignoring this unsociable opening. "Is she all right?" "Will she be here tomorrow?"

187

Gee, they hoped it wasn't too bad. Poor Mrs Rose. Perhaps if she went to bed for the day ... "What's she going to call her baby?"

"Does she want a boy or a girl?"

"It's better to have a boy first, because ... "

"Be quiet at once," I ordered. I had my "word", as I had promised to do, but I knew it was a waste of time. They were not in a mood receptive to corrective words. The whole form was aggrieved, partly at Jenny's punishment, partly at Mr Good's unkind remarks (quite unjustified, of course. Why, they hadn't even left their seats. They were *good*. They had just talked quietly and eaten their lunch.) – and partly because they had that morning at assembly learned the results of the term's form competition.

The form competition, based on marks for behaviour, uniform, tidiness of room and desks, took place each term, and the winning form had the privilege of having a Degas ballet picture hung above their blackboard for the next twelve weeks. H3C had again come sixteenth out of sixteen. They expected this, and were not indignant at the result. What hurt them was that in the uniform inspection, for which they had carefully prepared all interval by sponging out spots on their gym dresses, and straightening their ties and spitting on their handker-chiefs to clean their shoes – in the *uniform* inspection, they had lost marks for talking and jostling while in line. This had nothing whatever to do with uniform. A uniform inspection didn't mean behaving. They had said it was *uniform*. H3C were always ready to suffer in an orthodox way for their misconduct, but these side effects were considered a flagrant injustice. It was definitely "not fair". It was not as though they could help their bad behaviour, so it should not have been taken into account in a uniform inspection. *Uniform*, they had said, *uniform*.

Their continual misconduct was to them an Act of God, something to be sorry about, certainly, but quite outside their own control. And they were genuinely sorry about it. They were quite sympathetic towards the teachers whom they caused to suffer. It was real, not crocodile, tears, which they shed as they devoured their victims.

They were particularly sorry, I think, for Miss Harris, whom they treated shockingly, and of whom they were quite fond. She had again that morning complained to me of their behaviour, so I mentioned this as I continued to scold them. They looked very sad.

"Yes, it's a shame," agreed Susan. "We're awful in her class, and she's so nice."

"Gee yes, she's real nice."

"Then why," I protested, "are you so naughty for her? Pamela, whatever made you squirt ink at her skirt? Oh yes, I've heard about it, you naughty girl."

"I don't know," sighed Pamela. "I just wanted to at the time. I *am* sorry. But she says it's come out all right."

"She had to take it to the dry cleaner's," I said, "and that cost her eight and sixpence."

"Gee, that's a shame," said Pamela sympathetically.

"My mother spilt tomato sauce right down her new dress last week," said Denise.

"Never mind that now. If you like Miss Harris, why don't you show her by making a real effort to behave better? You can do it if you try. She *is* nice, as you say, and yet you behave so badly in her class. She's always sticking up for you people, too." This was a downright lie, as the gentle Miss Harris had that morning observed to me how pleasant it would be to consign them all to a treadmill for the rest of their natural life. But it worked. There was silence.

Then "*Does* she?" unbelievingly.

189

"Of course she does. And you know how good she has been to you – remember how she helped you in the form basketball contest by all those extra practices?"

Gee, yes, they remembered. She *was* nice to them.

"Now why don't you do something for her in return by showing her that you really *can* behave?"

I had not expected any good result to come of this – I had learned never to expect any good from my reproaches to H3C. But the next day Miss Harris approached me with a dazed expression.

"Whatever's the matter with H3C? Are they all sickening for scarlet fever? They were quite good this morning. Every time one of them started to talk the others shushed her. Whatever's got into them?"

H3C were also dazed – at their own virtue. They hadn't known this could happen to them.

"We were *good*," they told me proudly, "real good. And we're going to be good next time, too."

They were, but this was the most they could manage.

"We weren't good at all this morning for Miss Harris," they told me sadly the day after. "We were just aaaawful again. Gee, it was a shame."

Chapter 12

The staffroom atmosphere was more than usually tense, and there was a noticeable uneasiness among the teachers. The inspectors were about to pay us a three-day visit.

Inspectors are intrepid individuals who, through a self-destructive urge, an inner voice, or a handful of silver, abandon their normal way of life and their loved ones, and join the Inspectorate Division of the Department of Education. From then on, they are sad and lonely souls who paddle joylessly in a sea of mistrust. Their arrival is preceded by ripples of dread; they leave dejection in their wake.

Between teacher and inspector exists a mutual lack of confidence. They meet with outward geniality, but are in fact mentally approaching each other with the wary watchfulness of two tomcats in a potato patch.

Communication is awkward. If you sit down beside an Inspector at morning tea, to talk about the cricket test, you may be thought to be seeking undue influence. If you avoid him, you may be marked low on the "relations with colleagues" section. Entertainment of inspectors is usually left in the hands of the Headmaster, the First Assistant, and others of a grade which no longer suffers inspection.

As they have been teachers themselves, it is natural for inspectors to believe the worst. If all your books are nicely marked up to date, they suspect you of having done it all the night before, as you probably did. If your lesson flows smoothly in copybook fashion from "recapitulation of previous day's work" to "revision of new material presented", they decide that it has been worked up and put on especially for their benefit, as it no doubt has. If the class know the answers to your questions, they think you are cheating by giving the same lesson for the third day on end, but here they are wrong. Even if you did resort to such a strategem, you would never get away with it.

To school inspectors, as to all creatures cut off from a normal healthy life, Nature has offered certain compensatory gifts. They develop some strange additional senses. They are able, for instance, to stand for a moment in the doorway of a classroom they have never seen before, and then, by some weird unerring instinct, walk straight to the worst book in the class. They can judge their moment of entry to such a nicety that they come into a room at the precise moment when you are attempting to answer offhand a question which has nothing to do with the lesson.

"Just carry on," they remark.

"We were running through the difference between a simile and a metaphor," you say. (You're pretty hot stuff on that.)

"Oh no we weren't," interrupts your front row. "Robert had just asked you to explain why that horse his father backed on Saturday was disqualified, remember?"

They sit down beside the very pupil who has today returned to school after a fortnight's absence with the measles, and ask him confidentially what he knows about the subject under discussion. The pupil, who has already told the teachers and the pupils about his grave illness and his near escape from death, now looks blank and says nothing at all.

As I did not intend to continue teaching for long, the inspectors' visit at first left me unmoved, except for the agreeable surprise of finding that we had hot scones for morning and afternoon tea. Had I only known it, it was the most important inspection of my own teaching career, as the initial marks for teaching ability are the ones on which subsequent grading is based. But of this I was happily unaware, and welcomed the inspectors as a possible source of help in solving various problems of presentation and method. I did not know then, either, that willing though the inspectors are to help and advise, their itinerary leaves little time for this. On one occasion four years later, I spent three days trying to locate and fasten down a visiting modern languages inspector in order to settle a tricky point of grammar. Each time I waylaid him he would look flustered and protest "Oh yes yes, certainly, but I'm due now at room sixteen and I'm already late . . . " or "Yes, by all means, but excuse me now – Mr L. is waiting . . . " He was very polite and very busy. I finally made an arrangement through the Headmaster to see this particular inspector before he left the school. On the last day, just before his departure, he bustled up to me while all the other inspectors were waiting in the car with the engine running. "You wanted to see me urgently, Mrs Bream?" I put my difficulty, and explained why I had no other source of information. He did not know the answer – this was not his fault. Nor was he to blame for having been unable to see me sooner. But time had been wasted for us both.

To the young graduates on the staff, the visit was frightening. Inspection meant grading, grading in turn affected salary and prospects for advancement. Their alarm and apprehension were infectious, and I found that I could not remain indifferent for long. In fact it seemed as discourteous not to show a certain amount of despondency as it would have been to prepare without more than usual care. We had to fight this invasion as a team and a united team we were. However kind and understanding inspectors are, they remain the Enemy, serving at least to unite the teaching staff for this brief spell into a firmer fellowship and co-operation than has previously existed. We lent one another wall maps and charts to cover the "use of visual aids" requirement; in periods when we knew the inspectors of our own subject were in conference, or in town, we secretly housed in our own rooms particularly troublesome children from other classes; we spoke soothing words of encouragement to one another at interval; and at every disaster we agreed that it was a shame, that the inspector would surely not be influenced by such an abnormal situation, and that the whole system stank anyway, and who cared? It was very comforting. And we enjoyed the hot scones, arriving promptly the first two days and cleaning them all up before the inspectors entered the staffroom. Miss McComish, who had been given the duty of inspector-feeding, discovered this, and subsequently hid the plates in a cupboard in the kitchen, until the First Assistant, her accomplice, sent her word that the moment – and the inspectors – had come. The staff regarded this as a dirty trick.

After school, when the inspectors had left for home, we would relate our woes to one another and compare misfortunes.

"They're mean," complained Miss Harris. "Mean, mean, mean."

"The inspectors?"

"No, those wretched boys in 4T2. They told me they

had to leave class at two o'clock for that football photo – while *he* was there – then they were sent back because they weren't supposed to go until two-fifteen. And *he* thought it was my fault. They knew it was two-fifteen, I bet they did."

"I hadn't marked the social studies notebooks," said Mr Limmer, the teacher from England. "They commented on it. I will not mark social studies notebooks. Why should I? I mark their homework assignments. I mark English exercise books, I mark arithmetic, but I do not mark social studies notebooks. There is a psychological barrier which prevents me from doing it."

"Did you explain that to the inspector?"

"No. I thought he might not understand."

"Well thank goodness for that. We all have that psychological barrier about marking. You had better make sure that he sees your best English books."

"How would you like it if a boy was hiding in a cupboard in your room for half the period?" asked Miss Tulley. "Yes, while the inspector was there. In the dressmaking room. I had to take 4T1 in there because Mr Henley's away. And Robert Morrison was in the cupboard for twenty minutes. He didn't dare come out because the inspector came in. Then the inspector finally turned his back on the class, and Robert emerged and slid into a seat."

"Did he notice?"

"The inspector? I don't know. He looked as if he was counting heads and found the addition a little puzzling, but he didn't say anything."

"I suddenly couldn't remember how to spell 'omission'," said Mr Hercus. "And I had to write it on the board."

"My bloke asked Marion Hertley in the sixth to comment on T.S. Eliot's outlook on life," said Mr King.

"She said 'Who's he?' And we spent three weeks on him last term! She told me after the lesson that of course she had heard of him, but she couldn't imagine what the Springbok tour had to do with English."

"Mine said 'I can see biology is your subject, not geography'. He saw me taking both. Is it good or bad?"

"That depends on which word he emphasised – was it NOT geography, or IS your subject . . . Where have those scones gone?"

"The brutes. They've eaten them."

No, the inspectors didn't have a chance. They tried to be understanding and friendly, but we regarded them as inquisitors or secret police, and attributed to their every action the worst of motives.

H3C had looked forward to the visit as something to break the monotony of school routine. They had no illusions as to who was being inspected. They were very sympathetic and out of sheer kindness made an effort to tidy up their English books. I had not asked them to do this – I would have preferred the English inspector to see H3C's books in their ragged, grease-spotted, natural state, and then tell me how to prevent them from reaching this condition. But tidying up was part of the routine. You always tidied up your books for the inspectors, said H3C. They had been told that in primary school. And could they do it in class, please? Some of them covered their books with floral wallpaper, and, in letters of various design and colour, wrote "English" on the outside – in most cases a flagrant lie, as the contents bore little resemblance to the promise of the title.

Jenny was happy, because she had a brand new book, unsullied by any writing at all. This was because Jenny had that term hit upon a new method of dodging spelling and grammar corrections, a chore which I demanded be done, and which Jenny disliked. She simply tore out the pages of her exercise book as she used them up. When I accused her of this, she denied it hotly, saying that all the exercises for correction were in another book, which she had handed up to Miss Burton at detention, and had not received back. She was aware that I did not believe this, even before checking with Miss Burton, but it was a good story. I then pointed out the slimness of her exercise book compared with others. She insisted that it had been that size since she first bought it from the school stationery shop. If that were so, I told her, she had better complain to the Principal that her book had less than half as many pages as anyone else's, and ask for her money back. She replied that she would be glad to, and was prepared to go there and then. I later consulted Mr Good. He was very angry, and sent for Jenny. I do not know what happened in that interview, but he had not met Jenny before, which perhaps explains why Jenny emerged with a happy smile, and why her book continued to become thinner and thinner until I threw it away. As it still had an uncorrected exercise in it at the time, Jenny did not resent this, and bought a new book to start afresh. I unkindly made her number the pages.

The English inspector was prompt, plump, and devastating. He criticised the exercise books, the blackboard, the textbook, the room, my promenade bench, the arrangement of desks, my teaching, and Lynn's hair, all, I think, with justification. I liked him, and so did H3C. They made room for him to sit down, and greeted him in a friendly, if unimpressed manner, then ignored him and continued to behave in their normal way. I did not mind this, as they were never unruly in my classes now – simply inattentive and lazy. In Mr Hughes's inspection period they took advantage of the conversation between the inspector and Mr Hughes to substitute comics for their textbooks, comb one another's hair, finish their dressmaking diagrams, and unscrew the backs of two chairs. This did not make a very good impression on the inspector. Mr Hughes was furious with them and kept them in after school for a week when the inspectors had left. H3C were indignant – why, they had hardly talked at all – they had been *good* – they hadn't left their places once! The same man visited my School Certificate English class, but he was less welcome here, as he told me in a voice which he no doubt thought was a whisper, but which was perfectly audible to the two front rows, that I really mustn't expect much from this type of child, and that their chances of passing were slim. This gave a further downward push to the already pessimistic attitude of the form, and my efforts to explain it away afterwards were unsuccessful.

H3C were a little worried on my behalf about the coming inspection of social studies.

"You're not very good at geography, are you?" asked Denise, the day before their visit.

"No, Denise, I'm not, but we shan't worry about that."

"What will he do to you if he's not pleased?" said Heather.

"I know," said Julie, "you tell us what to learn the day before and we'll learn it like anything and show the inspector."

"Julie, every single day I have told you what to learn the day before, and just how often do you do it?"

"We will but. We really will."

"You could just ask us things we know," suggested Yvonne.

"Like what?" said Julie. I was privately asking myself the same question – like what? The things H3C knew were not the sort of topics to be brought into a decently run social studies lesson.

"We must all know *something*," said Lynn. "I heard once where an inspector was coming and all the pupils put up their hands and if they knew they put up their right hand and if they didn't they put up their left anyway. And the inspector thought what a clever class, because all the hands were up."

"*You*'d get all muddled, Lynn," said Denise.

"Now stop this discussion at once," I interrupted. "It is nice of you to want to help me, but we must have no deception at all. The inspector is coming in to see exactly how you are getting on with your social studies, and that is just what we shall show him. And perhaps he can help me by showing me new ways to teach you. It will be very useful to have him with us, and there is to be no pretence of knowing what you don't. Just behave nicely and be polite."

But H3C's shameful suggestions began to influence me. I would certainly not deceive the inspector in the manner they recommended. But why must I conduct before him a lesson in a subject which still confused me, a subject which I had never offered to teach nor wanted to teach? Why should my teaching ability be judged while it was handicapped by ignorance? So when, later in the lesson, Julie asked, "What day are we going to give those talks we had to prepare?" I succumbed without any struggle to the opportunity presenting itself, and promptly replied, "Tomorrow. When the inspector is here. Who will go first?"

H3C did not suffer from shyness. There were several volunteers, and I chose Gail, whose father kept a market garden, and who proposed to tell us about growing vegetables. I hoped this had something to do with social studies, for the syllabus seemed to be generously wide. The next day, when the inspector arrived, Gail was already standing in front of the class, brandishing a hoe, which she had brought from home for the occasion, and showing her fellow pupils how to use it.

"Carry on, carry on," said the inspector. "I'll just stand here and listen in."

The class thought the time had now come to do their bit for school and teacher. They made a really admirable effort to be Interested and Intelligent.

"What do you do for blight on carrots?" asked Diane, as though she really cared. Fortunately Gail knew.

"Do you dig round lettuces to give them firm hearts?" enquired Susan. Gail, at a rough guess, said yes, that was right, you did.

The inspector stayed only a few minutes; then, I was told later, he sought out the Head of the Social Studies Department and burst into enthusiastic praise of my teaching methods. "That's the way I like to see the subject taught – getting the expert in the class to tell the others." He even remarked that other social studies teachers in the school might benefit from observing my lessons, a suggestion which sent the Department Head into spasmodic giggles for days afterwards.

But alas, that inspector just couldn't leave well alone. The next day, while I was still congratulating myself, and enjoying my ill-deserved success, he reappeared. He wanted to see some more of my class and its work, he told me. He had been most impressed, yes, *most* impressed, with what I was doing. He radiated approval and beamed with camaraderie. That was before he picked up Denise's book. I had marked Denise's work a fortnight ago, but since then her friends appeared to have been short of paper for darts. It now contained a photograph of Elvis Presley, a recipe for ginger muffins, and five pages of ziggurats.

The inspectors were with us only a few days, but they

left behind them a nervously exhausted staff. Minds were tired and tempers inflammable. And that is probably why, on July 27 at 11.15 a.m., Mrs Donning lined up all the girls in the fourth form art class and caned them on the legs.

"You didn't!" gasped the First Assistant. "Oh no no no! You couldn't have! What the blazes are we in for now?"

"Provocation is your best defence," said Mr Bowron. "You were goaded beyond endurance and in the heat of the moment you hit out while temporarily of unsound mind."

"I was goaded beyond endurance," said Mrs Donning calmly, "but that process took all year. I did not retaliate in the heat of the moment. I did it coolly and deliberately, after several days' malice aforethought, and after due warning to the pupils. And I was of unsound mind only before I thought of it. At the first welcome whack my sanity was miraculously restored. It was beneficial to all concerned, and I have no regrets at all. The children behaved very well for the rest of the lesson, and I felt much better. I think I'll do it again tomorrow. In fact daily."

"You most certainly will not," said Mr Good. "There may not even be a tomorrow for you. Good God, woman, don't you realise what you've done? And wherever did you get the cane?"

"Oh that was yours," replied Mrs Donning happily. "You weren't in your office, so I borrowed it. It's returned quite safely," she assured him.

"And on the legs!" groaned the First Assistant. "Why, not even boys may be caned on the legs."

"Well, where else could I do it? I teach them art – they can't draw pretty flowers with sore hands. And I could hardly put them in a row and say 'Bottoms up!' You're making far too much of it. It was only one little hit each – not even very hard. Just to show them they're not really immune."

"But they *are* immune, Mrs Donning," protested Mr Good. "That's the point. Don't you see what you've started? Quite apart from all the possible lawsuits, there'll be letters to the newspapers, the Board will have to answer questions . . . Telephone calls will begin just as soon as those girls get home. I'm going out for the evening – and when I come home I'll leave my receiver off. I just don't know how we're going to get you out of this."

"They might not dare to tell their parents."

"Others will tell them. It'll be all over town by tonight."

"Well, I congratulate you, Mrs Donning," said Mr Hughes. "Caning is legalised for boys, and has proved to be satisfactory."

"Bah!" said Mr Robertson. "Caning is a shabby, antiquated punishment. It encourages aggressiveness, it is destructive to the character, it is an affront to the dignity of both master and pupil. It is a primitive and barbaric means of control which belongs only to the past."

"Do you use it?"

"Yes."

"Why?"

"I have to – self-defence. They'd walk all over me if I didn't. But I don't *like* it."

"The boys do, in preference to other punishments."

"That merely proves its ineffectiveness."

"Oh it's effective," admitted Mr Watts, "as a deterrent. That's it's only justification."

"There is no justification for it whatever," said Miss McComish. "The theory of Rousseau and others is that a child should simply suffer the natural consequence of his actions."

"Well, adult anger *is* a natural consequence to the actions of 4 Ag.," said Mr Hughes. "So they will continue to suffer if they give me cheek."

"It arouses hostility."

"It dispels *my* hostility."

"It is degrading."

"Of course it is – it's meant to be. That is surely its aim. To degrade the criminal as an example to others. The more degrading the better."

"It breeds resentment."

"Not as much as missing football practice. Most of 'em don't resent it at all – a sudden sharp pain instead of being deprived of an hour's rolling in the mud – they will settle for the cane any day."

"But it's a deliberate attack on another human being. Caning of boys is legal in schools, but if you did half as much to an adult, you'd be had up for assault."

"If you did the same to an adult under half as much provocation it would be regarded as justifiable self-defence. If an adult behaved as any of 4 Ag. do, he would be locked up before we needed to cane him."

"But you're attacking a child. It's not even sports-manlike to hit your inferior in size and intelligence."

"Would you say a hunter in Canada shouldn't shoot at a pack of wolves just because they are less mentally able? Who is really the inferior in opportunity? One lone teacher armed with a cane to 'be used sparingly', or a pack of thirty-six frenzied young delinquents who have him at their mercy? What sportsmanship do they show?"

"You're right," said Mr Howe. "We are outweighed by force of numbers, and they don't fight to rules. Take 4 Ag. Their intelligence as a whole may be inferior, but their cunning and maliciousness combined with a complete disregard of the truth make them an opponent with more power than any teacher."

"But don't you men run the risk of becoming cane-happy?" asked Miss Tulley. "And supposing you have a migraine or a whitlow? Mightn't you be sharing some of your own pain with a boy out of sheer bad temper? You wouldn't do it consciously, but there's always that risk. How can you be sure you're not being vindictive when you cane?"

"We probably are, and with just cause. Isn't that part of a pupil's general education? They must learn to adjust to other people's failings. They suffer from our moods, as we do from theirs. We are less patient at times; their behaviour fluctuates with the weather."

"It may be useful for them to learn when to expect more snarling than usual. But it's our job, as persons in command, to control our own moods so that they don't influence our teaching. If we can't, we shouldn't have the opportunity to cane, or to order a caning."

"Well, I like caning," said Mrs Donning happily. "Caning's nice. I feel good now. I'm going to cane some more. Lots more."

"You keep out of this argument. You're emotionally disturbed and therefore unable to state your case at the moment. Besides, you will be leaving the profession shortly. So just have another cup of coffee and be quiet."

"Will they publicly defrock her?" asked Miss Burton. "Or just give so many days for assault?"

"Might I remind you," said Mr Good wearily, "that the bell for afternoon school sounded several minutes ago, and none of you has yet moved in the direction of your class? One of the primary rules of good control . . . ''

When I reached my room H3C had tired of waiting in the corridor and had gone inside. Elaine was trying to sing louder than Sheryl. Heather was leaning out the window to pick up a ruler, while Diane held her by the legs. Denise was drawing pictures on the board. Susan was combing up Carolyn's hair. The rest were walking about, talking, except for Raewyn, who had her books out and was trying to work amid the hubbub.

"Get to your seats at once," I said. When they were settled I apologised for being late, but scolded them for not waiting quietly.

"How would you like it if I were to strap you all?"

"Like Mrs Donning," they grinned. So they already knew.

"I'm not permitted to," I said, "or else I probably would. But how do you feel about it? Do you think boys should be caned and not girls? Do you think there should be no caning at all?"

Opinions were divided. Heather and others thought the strap was the best punishment for girls, and told me how you could raise interesting blisters to make the teacher sorry, by coating your hand first with onion juice. All objected to the cane for girls, but only because the cane was associated with one portion of their body which they preferred not to be hit.

4 Ag. were nearly all in favour of caning for boys. It was quick, they said, they didn't like it, but they forgot it a few hours later.

I asked all my classes, but none were of help to me in forming my own opinion on corporal punishment in schools. A cane is a dangerous toy in the wrong hands or at the wrong time. It is admittedly barbaric. Yet it is effective. I asked myself which did the most permanent harm to the attitude and character of a pupil – the cruel biting sarcasm of Mr Lockhead, whom they feared and could not fully understand, or the heavy caning strokes of Mr Rowlings, of whose genuine affection and concern for them they were never in doubt. I was glad that I had no decision to make on the subject. I was not allowed by law to hit a girl, so I had no question to solve.

We waited with anxiety for the complaints against Mrs Donning to begin. She too was worried next day. The exhilaration had worn off, and the consequences of her action had been pointed out only too plainly and emphatically by Mr Good and the Principal. But days passed and still nothing happened. Then one phone call was received. The caller asked to speak to Mrs Donning. He warmly congratulated her on her method of dealing with his daughter, assured her that she had his full support, and invited her to repeat the punishment any time she wished. But she never did it again.

Chapter 13

The third term began with a smell of washed and disinfected floors. The desks had been sanded and varnished in some of the rooms (not mine, alas), and one corridor had been repainted. We gathered in the staffroom, congratulating ourselves, more than one another, on the fact that nearly all had returned. There was in fact only one change of personnel – quite a record, I was told. Mrs Rose had left now, and her place was taken by an eager youngster in his early twenties. He could not yet have met his classes, as he was still smiling. We welcomed him but bemoaned his sex, as there was now one woman fewer for duty.

Miss Burton, who only four days ago had shown me her written resignation, looked healthy and energetic. Mrs Donning was laughing merrily, and Miss Tulley was tidying up the shelves with a bustling vigour. I have always admired the remarkable precision with which have been calculated the occurrence and the duration of secondary school holidays. It must have taken gifted psychologists years of research into the breaking-strain of teachers and their degree of resilience, before they could have determined with such amazing accuracy the exact amount of recuperation leave necessary to maintain a school staff in workable condition. It takes only two weeks in May, three in August, and seven at the end of the year, yet the pattern of recovery is in each case the same.

Examine the August holidays, for example. During the first week, your body only has left the school. Your mind still spins with a discordant medley of Helen's report, Gregory's failure to understand parsing, that imposition you neglected to collect from Sharon, how to present the Victorian novelists, ways to combat Gary's dislike of verse, what a mistake it was to refer John to the science master ... In the fitful sleep allowed to you at night, you fail to solve long insoluble algebraic equations, enormous desks fall on top of you, you chase pupils, or the Headmaster, down unending corridors lined with basketballs which roll under your feet. And you snore. During the second week the worst of your nervous twitches begin to disappear, your forehead loses its taut binding pain, the throb in your head lessens a little. You can read simple light fiction now, and stroll moodily round the shops, but you are still too exhausted physically to accept invitations, or to entertain. In the third week you begin to take an interest in the world around you. You meet a few friends, tidy the garden, make some summer frocks. And you finally summon up enough energy to write out your resignation. For your common sense is flowing back and you know that no job on earth is worth what you lost last term in sanity and vigour. On the second to last day of the holidays you realise that you cannot face the coming school week. A pity you left it so late to resign, because you have the two requisite months to get through before you can be released. You can't manage it, of course. You will have to take sick leave – a pity, you don't like doing that. On the last day you feel a little better. Perhaps you could stick it out after all – for just two months. You get your books together and prepare a few lessons. And on the morning that school starts, the process of your recovery is suddenly complete. What a silly idea that was of resigning. You step briskly back to the battle line, full of hopes and plans and resolutions. This term will be better. And you won't let it get you down, either. Relax, that's the thing, just relax and don't care. Of course from the moment you step inside the school door the deterioration process is again set in motion, but of this you are unconscious, and you greet your colleagues and pupils with enthusiasm, as the cycle begins anew.

H3C arrived at my room smiling. They had found the three weeks' holiday quite long enough. Joanne came up to me as they filed in and said "I know about the girls that are missing."

"Yes, the class is smaller now, Joanne, isn't it? Go to your seat."

There were four gaps. Julie had finally run away from her foster parents, had been picked up in Dunedin, and was now in a detention home. Christine was staying in Waimate for a fortnight, minding a baby. Beverley was doing domestic work, while she waited to have one. Edith had turned fifteen and was working in Woolworths. But the rest of the class greeted me with cheerful, noisy enthusiasm. Some had even found the holidays "boring". They approved my new skirt and thought that it would go good with that blue jumper I had with the two white stripes. I said I would wear them together on the next cold day.

Carolyn's hair was now auburn. I did not think it improved her looks, but I was in the minority. In fact I *was* the minority. I could see from the admiration shown that there would be several auburn competitors for Carolyn in the coming weeks. Felicity had had her long pigtails removed. She looked sweet and pretty with a fringe and a short bob, but I hoped that she would not too badly miss her pigtails, which she had been accustomed to cling to as if for support, and occasionally to chew. We all admired her short hair, however, and she smiled broadly. Shirley and Helen had become blondes, Jane had adopted a pony tail. Pamela's arm was in a sling, through her falling off the back of a truck, and we sympathised with her because it was the left one, and therefore no homework or school work would be excused. Elaine was wearing red shoes, because "Mum says it's no use buying any more black ones because I'll be fifteen in November and then I'm leaving."

"Gee, isn't she lucky?" said Lynn.

"What are you going to do when you leave, Elaine?"

"Work in Preston Shirts."

"Are you looking forward to it?"

"Gee yes."

For most of our girls, the fifteenth birthday was a radiant goal to be reached – shining like a symbol of freedom before them, the day on which they would cease to be directed by the sound of a bell, and work far harder to the call of a whistle. They would have money, real money, of their own, they could buy clothes of their choice, and wear as much make-up as they pleased. An eight-hour day of a mechanical, tiring job seemed to be a small price to pay for such delights. As H3C were older than most third-formers, I had often tried to discuss with them the advantages of staying at school. But few saw any point in remaining one day longer than necessary. Not many would reach fifteen this year, and they envied Elaine. Yet I knew that Elaine would probably work a few weeks at Prestons, then drift to another job, then another. That was so often the pattern. But she would not regret leaving school. Raewyn alone of them dreaded the day she must leave.

Joanne put up her hand. "I know where the missing ones are."

"Do you, Joanne? Have you heard from Julie?"

"No." No one had heard from Julie.

"She'll be happier in a home," said Heather. "Much happier than when she was here. She used to cry and cry. Those people didn't like her – they just took her for the money."

"I know a girl who was in a detention home," said Susan, "and they used to hit her with a piece of board."

"That's not true," said Carolyn. "My cousin was at Waikeria for two weeks and he said it was good fun."

"It is so true. This wasn't Waikeria and they hit her with a piece of board."

"Well, she must have tried to run away. Or else it's not true."

"Hush, both of you. Has anyone heard from Beverley?"

Helen had. Beverley had written to say where she was working, but little else.

"You get girls cheap when they're going to have a baby," Denise told us all. "My aunt she married a store boss and she's well off and she has a maid and she always gets one of them if she can. Only *she's* nice to them – gives them things and all."

We all hoped that Beverley was working for people who were nice, like Denise's aunt who married the store boss, and that she was not too unhappy about having a baby.

"They won't even let her keep it," said Sally. "They make people adopt them."

"Not always they don't. My cousin kept hers."

We had a brief discussion on the trials of unmarried mothers.

Most of the girls had been to Woolworths to see Edith.

She was enjoying her work, they told me. She wore a little tag with her number on, and was real good at change now.

"I know about the ones missing," said Joanne. "Mum said to tell you."

"Did she, Joanne? Have you seen Edith too?"

"Yes."

"And have you heard from Christine?"

"No."

"Well, we had better do some work now. Take out your English books."

But not many of H3C had brought a book. Bring books on the first day of term? I had not really expected it.

"Can we write an essay on our holidays?" asked Carolyn.

"Do you really want to?" This was a subject which I never set for an essay, through memories of my own school days when each holiday, film, picnic, or outing, was inevitably clouded by the certain knowledge that it would have to be described in writing during the next English period.

But nearly all the class were anxious to give an account of their holidays, and so I let them express themselves in an essay, with, for once, no restriction on the length. I usually made them confine their essays to one page, which must be carefully checked and punctuated. It was the only way, I had found, to effect any improvement in their written expression. But today I allowed them to write freely, for satisfaction rather than exercise in English, and most of them handed up several pages at the end of the period. There was no literary value in them, but they had enjoyed writing them, and the essays made interesting reading. They were not as frank as their letters to Jeannette had been, but they gave some indication of the means they had adopted to find relief

212

from the boredom and the domestic unhappiness of their homes. Some were pathetically imaginative, describing as accomplished what the writer would have liked to do. Some girls had gone to Australia, some had won beauty contests, a few had met handsome boy friends and been to dances in lovely new dresses.

4 Ag. came in happily too. They had all enjoyed their holidays, and several had had the opportunity to work on farms, an arrangement made in most cases by their agriculture teacher. As the standard of their English was fairly high, I decided we could afford the time to discuss what was far more important to them, and in turn they told the class of their experiences on the farms. There were many technical terms and farming procedures which they had to stop and explain to me, and this was done with enthusiasm. Hugh had left and was now at Rangiora High School, where they had a real model farm, which he had been allowed to walk around in the holidays. He described it in a letter which Brian read aloud, and all were envious of the conditions in which Hugh would be working this term. Agriculture was a real and vital course to most of these boys, and they were at least fortunate that in our paved area where nothing resembling a farm was ever in sight, they had an inspired and hard working teacher who arranged as much practical experience for them as was possible.

I rejoined the staff for morning tea. We talked mainly of school, and school pupils, and lessons, as teachers are prone to do, but after a while Mrs Donning remarked casually, "I wonder what has happened to the girls that are missing?"

"Three from my form," said Miss Burton. "All working in factories."

"You're lucky," said Miss Tulley. "Mine have all come back, and I just can't teach a class of thirty-eight as I would like to teach."

"I can't teach any class as I would like to teach," said Miss Harris.

"I mean those two girls that are missing," said Mrs Donning. "The ones that ran away." We looked blank. "Don't you read the morning paper?"

Several of us had not had time to look at it before school.

"Not our girls, thank goodness," explained Mr Hughes. "They were both sixteen, so they must have left school. They haven't been seen since yesterday morning."

In the depths of my dull confused memory, something began to stir.

"Joanne!" I exclaimed suddenly, and jumped up, spilling my tea.

I found Joanne in the playground, trying to push a broken ballpoint up one of the drinking taps. Yes, she knew about the girls who were missing. Mum had said she must tell me. They lived near her and they had told her on Saturday night, as a secret, where they were going. She had promised not to tell. But Mum said she must break her promise and tell me. I led her in to Mr Newall, reflecting that it was not only H3C who needed to be told a fact at least three times before they took notice.

By the time I had seen Mr Newall, and left Joanne with him, I was nearly ten minutes late for my next class, the fifth form English group. They looked at me reproachfully, and one said "We thought there must be no one to take us." Last term, I knew, this would have been a matter for rejoicing, not complaint, and I looked around at strangely attentive faces. 5HT were a changed class. In three weeks they had been transformed from lazy, inattentive, carefree idlers, to earnest and worried students. For the nebulous remote School Certificate

214

had now become sudden reality. There were only a few weeks to go, and a year's work to do. One boy had realised this in the holidays. After refusing to work all year, failing to do his homework for me, and being a nuisance and a distraction in all my fifth form English classes, he had had a burst of energy, probably under parental pressure, and had posted to me a fat package of exercises which he had done from his textbook, with a brief note attached to them: "Please mark these and send them back." I was annoyed, but perhaps he had thought to please – after all, I had been begging him and ordering him to work all year. I could not discourage his belated effort, and so I had spent two whole days of my holiday in marking his work.

For most of the class, I knew that this improvement in attitude had come too late to bring success, and as the weeks passed after that day it became increasingly distressing to watch their pitiable efforts to make up lost time. They had all brought their books for this first lesson of the term, and that in itself was a strange occurrence. Several had exercises to be marked, and there was an eagerness for knowledge which I had never seen in them before. Only Alice, who had worked steadily all year, was unworried. She had not worked in the holidays – she had gone away for the whole three weeks and had a very enjoyable time staying with her cousins on a farm. The others looked at her with distaste.

In the afternoon I had a social studies lesson with H3C, and for this I had not prepared. This is never a wise omission. I had already learned by now two of the fundamental rules for taking a lesson: firstly, to know beforehand exactly what you intend to do, and secondly, not necessarily to do it. I had several minutes to think, while they sat and settled. One always had several minutes to think, while H3C sat and settled. You could count on it. And during this time I remembered that I had not yet touched the civics section of their social studies syllabus. Perhaps I could give them a brief summary of the system of justice in New Zealand, and procedure of the law courts. That would be useful general knowledge and should interest them. It certainly did. We talked about the Magistrate's and Supreme Courts, about judges, offences and bail, and the class did most of the talking.

"They're nice to you when you're waiting for trial," said Heather. "My mother she even got breakfast in bed."

"Yeah, but that's only before the trial," said Jenny. "My brother – aw he did something silly and he got ten days – he didn't get breakfast in bed. No fear." She giggled.

"You don't ever get breakfast in bed in prison," said Diane. "You line up with a plate. And you're woken at six o'clock to tidy your room."

"The meals are good but," volunteered Carolyn. "My brother says they fed him better than Mum did. Gee Mum was cross at that."

"The showers are the worst, my uncle says," said Helen. "You have to have a shower every morning."

"You do not," said Susan. "That's only before you go to prison – while you're waiting."

"My brother didn't have to have a shower every day," said Carolyn. "Gee he'd have told us that if he'd had to. He wouldn't have liked that."

"Well I bet he did so have to," argued Helen. "My uncle says you have to and he ought to know."

"Well Carolyn's right. You don't have to," interposed Jane. "I know you don't because my father . . . "

There was no embarrassment or reticence as they exchanged information, and recounted the experiences of their jailed relatives. My knowledge of certain details of court procedure and prison routine was greatly enlarged by the end of that lesson, but I don't think I had taught much to my class.

Because Mrs Rose and her replacement did not teach the same subjects, the timetable was unsettled, and Miss Harris and I decided to exchange for the last period of this first day the classes we had been allotted. This would give her my sixth form supervision, which I thought would be boring, and relieve her of H3C, whom she found exasperating at all times. We agreed to go to each other's room for that period, rather than move the classes.

H3C arrived – I could hear them coming two corridors away, and gathering up speed and vocal volume as they approached. They whooped into the room with Indian war screams, then stopped in amazement as they saw me waiting. I sent them back to come in again. They entered slightly more quietly and I felt rather sorry for them. They liked Miss Harris, and had probably been looking forward to having this last period with her. I felt obliged to apologise to them for taking them a third time in one day.

"Gee, we *like* you taking us," Denise assured me. "Don't we?"

"Yes," said Heather. "You make us be good."

They all beamed assent and I knew that they meant it. I certainly did not "make them be good." No one could do that. But by taking them for two subjects, by having white hair, by expending much energy and nerve-racking effort, and by a great deal of good fortune, I now usually achieved a relatively minor degree of misbehaviour from them, which to H3C was a state of "being good." I had not known before that they actually enjoyed this mild and quite inadequate suppression, but I realise

217

now that it gave them a sense of safety and security – something many of their homes did not provide – and it relieved them of any responsibility for self-discipline. They really liked to be "good" if someone else did all the work in making them so.

We settled down to arithmetic, and as I had never taken H3C for this subject before, I had to confess to them that I could not add very well, and I might make a mistake. Sure enough it was not long before I did so, and they delightedly spotted it in my blackboard working. Their own addition was good, and like 3HTB they enjoyed mechanical arithmetic. The period passed fairly pleasantly.

The next day they told Miss Harris about their boisterous entry into her classroom, and the surprise of seeing me standing there.

"We had to behave all through the lesson," they told her untruthfully.

"Well, anyway," Heather said, "Mrs Bream can't add." At this criticism Colleen had risen to my defence. "How could you expect her to? She's an old lady."

All this was told me by the rest of the class in indignation at Colleen.

"You're not really old," they assured me, "so she shouldn't have said that. But she didn't mean it."

"No, I didn't mean you were old, truly I didn't," said Colleen in distress. "You're not old."

"That's all right, Colleen," I told her. "You haven't insulted me. I don't mind being old. I rather like it. So stop worrying about it."

"Oh, you're *not* old, Mrs Bream," they protested again. Their warm and wicked little hearts could not have me hurt by this fancied insult. "Not a *bit* old. And Miss Harris told Colleen that at least you're a lady and she only hopes each of us one day may manage to be

218

one."

I tried to convince them that I was not offended, and the lesson continued, but I could see that the matter still rankled. At last Pamela put up her hand.

"Yes, Pamela?"

"Look, Mrs Bream, if you're old my mother must be just *ancient*."

They were unusually attentive for the rest of the period.

Chapter 14

"Now look, Mrs Bream," said the First Assistant. "We must consider the cleaners."

I agreed readily. "I'm sure we must."

"They're not easy to get, you know."

"I suppose not."

"Of course it's easy to forget. We all do it. I've done it."

"Yes, forgetting is not really difficult when you've had a bit of practice."

"But you *will* be more careful in future, please."

"Mr Good, whatever are you talking about?"

"I told you – didn't I? The chairs, the chairs, Mrs Bream."

"Chairs?"

"It does so delay the cleaners when they're left down. You weren't the only one. Apparently three teachers forgot last night to have them put up."

"But the chairs in my room were put up at the end of the last period yesterday, Mr Good. I often *do* forget, but I didn't yesterday."

Mr Good looked at me with the expression I probably adopted on hearing one of Jenny's wild statements. He shook his head slowly.

"Not one, Mrs Bream. Not one single chair in your room had been put on a desk."

I did not, like Jenny, explode into vociferous denial. After all, I sometimes did forget the chairs and deserved the rebuke. But yesterday. . . yes it was Tuesday. 4 Ag. last period. As soon as I had closed the lesson, their kindly restraint in my room was considered at an end. They lifted the chairs high above their head and crashed them down on the desks in enthusiastic competition and deafening noise. School chairs must be sturdily built – I was always slightly surprised to find them still in one piece next morning. In a cowardly fashion, I used to leave the room at the first bang, but I could hear the ear-shattering performance continuing as I walked down the corridor and up the stairs. 4 Ag. not put up the chairs? Why, they wouldn't have missed it for anything less than a football match.

"And I'm giving you a student," continued Mr Good.

"Who, me? Oh no you don't. I have not yet learned even the rudiments of teaching. What help could I possibly be to a student? No thank you, no student. It was a nice kindly thought, but I decline."

"I'm afraid you are in no position to decline, Mrs Bream. You have no choice in the matter. Yours are the only English classes which fit in with her timetable. It's a young lady, a Miss Morgan. She will come to you for English with H3C, and I'm sure she will find it of benefit. You are well qualified academically, and you know your subject well."

"Whatever has that to do with taking H3C? I can't even control that mob, and as for teaching them anything . . . "

He listened to no more protests. He was still a little annoyed about the chairs, and we had by this time reached my room, from which came a sound of scuffles, shrieks, loud laughter and desks being scraped across the floor. H3C were in residence.

He winced. "I shan't detain you," he said, and turned into his office, shutting the door behind him.

As the class settled, I stood on my bench, considering. If I said, "Who took down the chairs?" no one would answer. If I said, "Did you put down the chairs?" all of them would answer. They would reply that of course they didn't, they wouldn't do that, it must have been those girls in the next room, or the caretaker, or some boys waiting for Mr Good. I had no doubt, of course, that only H3C would have taken them down.

"*Why*," I said finally, "tell me just *why* you took all the chairs off the desks last night."

There was silence, while they considered just how much I knew. Heather must have decided that there had been a witness, for after a while she spoke.

"We had to," she said, "because of Susan's clicker."

"What clicker, Susan? What do you mean?"

Susan put one hand in her blazer pocket and demonstrated. Click-clack-click came a tinny sound. It was familiar, and before Susan drew the object from her pocket I had identified it as one of those small metal crickets which are found in Christmas bonbons, and which give a sharp protest each time their stomach is squeezed.

"How did that clicker cause you to take down all the chairs, Susan?"

"Oh, I didn't, Mrs Bream. I only lifted three down, honest I did. I did, didn't I Heather? Didn't I, Shirley? True I did, only three."

"Mrs Bream," said Denise, "my aunt she's got one of those beaut new chairs with the footstool and they tip back when you ... "

"Be quiet, Denise." I continued with a slow extraction

223

of the facts. It had begun in science, the first period after lunch. Susan had clicked, Mr Hughes had confiscated. He had put the little cricket on his table and proceeded with the lesson, but when H3C had left, the cricket was no longer there. Susan had obviously taken it as she passed his table. Mr Hughes was very annoyed. He had had a trying lesson with H3C, and this was sufficient to break his patience. From Colleen, who as usual was the last to leave, he learned that the class was now going to my room, and he strode there angrily. I had a non-teaching period, and as the clothing room was undergoing alterations, Miss Tulley was using my room this period for her dressmaking lesson. Mr Hughes entered the room, expressed vividly his opinion of Susan, and demanded return of the cricket. Susan said she didn't have it. Mr Hughes ordered that she turn out her pockets, open her case and desk. No cricket. Miss Tulley and he then conducted a thorough search of all desks, cases and pockets. No cricket. There was no cricket because as danger had begun to threaten Heather had with great presence of mind removed a piece of chewing gum from her mouth and passed it across to Susan with whispered directions. Susan reached one hand under her chair and fastened the cricket out of sight. Mr Hughes had accompanied Susan to her locker, searched it, and then apologised for his unfounded suspicions.

"Gee, I almost told him then," said Susan. "He was so nice."

"And you *will* tell him, Susan," I remarked. "I'll see you later about that."

"Yes, Mrs Bream," she agreed cheerfully. She knew that once Mr Hughes's anger had had time to abate, he was always easy-going. She would doubtless get off with a detention, and who cared about that? She would have her cricket safely off the premises by then.

It would have been simple enough to collect the cricket after school, had normal lessons taken place. But Miss Tulley had used the room for cutting out, which entailed putting desks together to make a large enough surface. Chairs had been shifted anywhere out of the way, and she and I had quickly lined them up again when I arrived to wait for 4 Ag. So to find the cricket Susan and her friends had to look under each chair. The chairs were standing upright on the desks, and rather than peer underneath them, it was easier to take them off, swing them over to look at the bottom, and then place them on the floor. I quite believed Susan's protest that she herself had moved only three. I was sure she had many willing assistants, for such a treasure hunt would have appealed to all the form. When every chair was down, someone found the cricket on the floor. The gum had failed to hold its captive.

I scolded the class, then changed the subject.

"We are going to have a student teacher in our English class shortly."

"Oh beaut." "What's she like?" "We had a man student last year." "Did she want to come here?" "Is she going to learn to be a teacher like you?"

I fervently hoped that the poor young lady would learn to be a teacher *not* like me, but I said, "Yes, that's right," and gave a little lecture on being polite and cooperative and obedient to students.

Two days later she arrived. She was a pretty blonde girl, whom I liked at once. She was self-effacing, intelligent, and sincere. H3C liked her too. They fetched a chair for her without being asked, and made her welcome.

"Are you learning to be a teacher?" I overheard. "Gee, whatever do you want to do *that* for?" H3C were full of sympathy for the teachers whom they were

225

gradually destroying, and could not imagine why anyone would willingly step into such an unenviable position.

For the first few days Miss Morgan sat at the back of the room and took copious notes on my lessons, which she afterward gave me to read. I was amazed at the interpretation which had been put on the haphazard course of my lessons.

"The point of the necessity for unaffected language and for clarity of expression," she wrote, "was emphasised and amplified very effectively at this point by a discussion on common swearing and profanity. This was introduced by the teacher to illustrate the uselessness of repetitive and meaningless phrases, and gave weight to her arguments in favour of simplicity."

"No, no, no," I protested. "It wasn't like that at all. The teacher hadn't planned anything of the sort. The teacher just happened to hear Lynn say, 'Take your bloody foot off my pencil case, Denise,'" and thought it advisable to intervene."

But Miss Morgan was unconvinced, and the next day her report read: "This lesson was an introduction to the Elizabethan stage and its dramatists. After a brief description of the theatre of that day, a contrast was made to present day drama by reference to the current radio serials which are most popular, and the difference in modern costuming was brought out by a class discussion on the dress worn in modern cinema productions . . . Doris Day and Ava Gardner were two examples quoted by the children . . . The lesson was competently rounded off by reference to the part taken by some of the pupils' relatives in amateur theatricals, the costume they adopted for their respective roles, and its subsequent disposal. By bringing the subject matter thus into the actual day to day lives of her pupils, the teacher gave point to her lesson, and helped to ensure recall of the salient facts."

Well, it had not happened quite like that. But I never really disillusioned Miss Morgan. Every incident in a lesson was twisted to fit into what could have been a carefully pre-arranged plan for the period. At last I gave up trying to convince her, and I let her write an account of the manner in which my lessons should have been planned and carried out, instead of the way they just bumped along. An outsider reading her notes would have been impressed by my planning, wisdom and foresight.

The next step was for Miss Morgan to take a lesson for me. This time it was I who sat at the back and took notes, with the aim of helping her. But her lesson was far better organised than any of mine – she needed no help from me there. Her only real difficulty of presentation was a failure to adjust her vocabulary to the limited understanding of H3C.

"Now your use of relative pronouns," she said gently, "will be facilitated if you just remember the rule that when the relative is the subject of the clause it introduces, it agrees with its antecedent in number and person."

"Huh?" said Pamela.

"I know," whispered Carolyn, who had previously asked me what the lesson was to be about. "It's 'who' and 'whose' and all that jazz."

Miss Morgan's manner with the girls was meek and kind and quite ineffectual. I had been instructed to leave her alone for brief periods with the class, to give her experience in controlling them alone, but each time I did so I waited in the corridor and the noise soon reached an unbearable fortissimo. I would hurry back into the room, to find a pale distraught Miss Morgan and a gleefully excited class.

"That's my whole trouble," she sighed. "I just can't

manage to keep pupils in order."

"None of us can keep H3C in order," I assured her. "They're passable for me only because I remind them of their grandmother and they think I'm too old and feeble to attack."

"But they won't even *listen* to me when you're not here."

"It doesn't really matter. You mustn't judge the school by this one class. We have some nicely-behaved ones, too."

"But I can't control *any* class, however good it is. I get dreadful marks for discipline, and quite good for everything else. They told me my control just must improve if I wanted a good report when I leave at the end of the year. This is my last school and they said they would watch for it carefully when they come to inspect me here."

"Cheer up. Most of the forms are quite good for students' 'crit.' lessons."

I was not very worried – anyone who hoped to control H3C had ambitions beyond normal human dreams. Miss Morgan begged me not to leave her alone with them again, and I didn't. She contented herself with helping in my class, or taking a lesson while I was present. H3C were very nice to her. They always had a chair ready, they lent her books, they audibly admired her dress and her hair style, and they told her about their families. She was a very welcome addition to our English classes, and a pleasant young companion for me.

Then the blow fell. Notice was received of the day and time of her "crit." lesson – the lesson which she must give before the Training College authorities and on which they would base their report of her teaching ability. To our dismay the class chosen was H3C. I was sure there must have been some mistake, and I hurried to Mr Good's office.

"Why ever has Miss Morgan been given H3C for her 'crit'? It's out of the question. Can you change it please?"

"Unfortunately, no. As a matter of fact, Mrs Bream" – he lowered his voice confidentially – "we were particularly asked to choose a troublesome class. She has so far had very bad reports for discipline and they want to see how she copes with the problems which arise. They don't expect her to subdue a difficult group, but they want to observe her methods, and judge whether her actual tackling of the situation has improved."

I was as alarmed as Miss Morgan – more so, perhaps, because she had some simple faith that H3C might be good on the day, whereas I happened to know how they had behaved in the first term, when Mr Hughes's student gave a "crit". lesson in science before them. The presence of Training College dignitaries had not deterred them in the least from throwing comics to one another, chewing gum visibly, and talking when they felt so inclined. And Yvonne, by twisting one foot round Diane's chair leg, and pulling steadily, had successfully tipped Diane onto the floor, at which the rest of the class roared and applauded. Mr Hughes when informed, had been furious, though the student, a cheery type, had not cared too greatly.

But Miss Morgan did care. She cared very much. I knew that H3C liked her, but then they liked all their teachers. This in no way improved their behaviour. A student giving a lesson was entirely at their mercy. Yes, she had reason to worry. I had an idea of secretly substituting one of the more amenable and quieter forms – I knew my friends on the staff would willingly co-operate – but as H3C had been so carefully chosen, I realised that any skulduggery in swopping would be soon discovered.

The matter seemed hopeless. Miss Morgan and I talked over possible schemes as we drank some strong black coffee.

"Just supposing you *could* control this particular class," I asked her, "would you then get a good report?"

"If I could control a class specially chosen like this one," she answered, "it would establish my discipline beyond any possible doubt. It would make all the difference to the report I leave Training College with. If *only* I could." She said "If only . . . " in the vague hopeless way one talks of winning the Golden Kiwi, or backing two successful outsiders in the double.

I was beginning to have an idea. I remembered how good H3C had been for me during the inspector's visit. I remembered their brief effort for Miss Harris. I remembered that before Mr Hughes's student gave his "crit.", Mr Hughes had threatened H3C with every punishment he could think of if they did not behave during the lesson. This was not quite the type of appeal to which H3C were tuned to respond. There was one method of approach, however, which might possibly work. And the only one.

"If it is really so important to you," I asked Miss Morgan, "are you willing to sacrifice a little dignity and prestige to have them quiet?"

"I'll sacrifice dignity and anything else, if they will only behave for that forty minutes."

The day before the "crit." lesson – it was no use my doing it earlier, as H3C's memories were short – I brought up the subject in social studies, which Miss Morgan did not attend with us.

"You like Miss Morgan, don't you?" I asked the class.

"Oh yes, she's nice."

"She went to Brisbane once."

"My aunt she married a store boss and he took her to

230

Tasmania and to Waiheke Island."

"She wears fab. dresses, doesn't she, Mrs Bream?"

"She's got nice hair."

"Peroxide."

"It is not."

" 'Tis so but. You can see the streaks."

"They're not streaks, are they, Mrs Bream?"

"Be quiet!" I ordered. "Now you like her, don't you?"

Yes, gee yes, they liked her a lot.

"She needs help tomorrow. Would you like to help her?"

Gee yes, they would all just love to help her. "*Can we?*"

I explained the whole situation to them. I told them about the "crit." lesson, about the Training College authorities' special interest, about Miss Morgan's difficulty in keeping any class under control.

"Ooooh yes," they agreed. "She can't manage us, anyway, she's too soft. We're just aaawful for her when you're not there."

I told them how much this "crit." lesson meant to Miss Morgan's career as a teacher, how the heads of the Training College would attend and watch carefully to see whether any of the pupils were talking or chewing or not attending – all of which would mean bad marks for a student – and whether the pupils were interested in what she was telling them and listening to her closely. I suggested how they could help. The idea appealed to them, probably as a novel masquerade out of character. They were soon full of enthusiasm. They were sure they could do it. They would listen hard and be very very attentive.

"It's only for one period," Heather reminded the others.

"And remember how good we were for Miss Harris

231

one day?" added Diane.

"*Two* days!" corrected the class indignantly.

Yes, of course they could do it. They were all eagerness to prove it. They could *so* keep it up for forty minutes! They would show me. They would be "as good as those clever ones in C3A".

I was not present at that "crit." lesson. Class teachers do not attend their students' trial. I waited anxiously in the staffroom, except for a brief tiptoed visit to the corridor outside the room. I could hear very little, and I dared not peep through the glass panel, but all seemed well, so I returned to what seemed a long wait. At last Miss Morgan came in, looking radiantly joyful.

"They were wonderful," she reported, "just wonderful. I know I'll get a good report now." She was glowing with happiness and relief as she described the lesson to me. The class had kept their promise, far even beyond our hopes. Not only had they been quiet and attentive while she spoke, but they had kept their eyes glued on her the whole time. They were careful to put their hands up and wait for an invitation before they spoke. (That in itself must have been a mighty effort for H3C.) And they were ready with questions. "Would you repeat that, please Miss Morgan?" – "Could you please tell us some more about Browning's early life?" – "What does 'inherited' mean? Thank you, I understand now." – "Do you mind if we copy that last bit down in our English books? It was so interesting." They surpassed even the "clever ones in C3A" in their attention, their interest, and their deep concern over the life and works of Robert Browning.

The trial was over, and success was sure. Miss Morgan presented me with a beautiful silk scarf, which was a surprise, but which I did not hesitate to accept gratefully, as I was feeling quite proud of my successful handling

232

of the problem.

H3C were proud, too. They glowed with virtue and self-congratulation. Never, never, had they been so good, they told me, and I quite believed them. I suspected too, that never never would they be so good again.

We all, H3C included, waited confidently for the report to arrive. At last Miss Morgan came to me one lunch hour waving it cheerfully – she had been waiting so that we could open it together and share the good news. We sat down to read it. "Preparation: excellent; Allocation of time: very good; Presentation of material: excellent; Voice: very good, a little soft perhaps, but clear and diction good; Blackboard use: excellent . . . " we hurried through all that – ah, here it was: "Discipline: it is most unfortunate that an assessment of the student's discipline cannot in this case be made. Control presented no problem during the lesson, as this particular class was an unusually docile one."

I was full of remorse, but what good did that do! My foolish mistake had ruined Miss Morgan's Training College report, had taken away the one chance she had left of an improved comment for control. I have never since interfered with a student's natural progress, but I often wear the ill-gotten scarf, and am reminded by it of my blundering crass stupidity.

Chapter 15

As the School Certificate examination drew near, our fifth form pupils worked and worried as never before. They realised now, as fifth-formers realise every year in every school, that a few frantic weeks are not quite enough in which to absorb three years' work. But in their newly receptive mood, they began to learn more easily. There was hope, and it became for them a race against time. My English group looked miserable and haggard, and my first question to them in a lesson was no longer, "Have you done your homework?" but, "What time did you go to bed last night?" I knew it was all their own fault. We had tried hard to persuade them to study earlier in the year, we had given up our own time after school and during lunch hours to keep them in and to try to force them to learn. They had only themselves to blame, I told myself, yet they were pathetic sights as the weeks passed. They arrived at school with heavy reddened lids and shadows which were no longer outwardly applied.

But the week before the examination began, they seemed to relax. Some had achieved this by simply giving up hope. Others admitted to taking sedatives. The father of one girl had bought a record which claimed to soothe and refresh, and they would gather in groups to listen to this. They played it for me. "You are about to receive your own thoughts," droned a deep voice. " . . . I breathe in deeeeply and I breathe out eeeeasily . . . " I found the foreign accent and the intonation more entertaining than soothing, but I encouraged them to use the record if it helped them.

Then came the day itself and the poor little victims disappeared from our sight. The examinations were held in our school hall, under visiting supervisors, but the candidates arrived when school had started and left when most of the other pupils had already gone home. We saw them crossing the playground at times, but they avoided us when possible.

School examinations took place about the same time, and when these were over the working year had also, in the opinion of the pupils, been formally closed. Lessons were difficult to take, we had to resort to play reading, debates, films and working parties.

Various functions took place. One afternoon the lunch hour sewing group handed over formally to a Corso representative, the work they had completed during the year. The sewing group had been an idea of Miss Ferguson. She had called a women's staff meeting and suggested it to us. "If you would care to help," she remarked mildly, "I would be glad to have the girls supervised each lunch hour. Let me see . . . you on Monday, Miss Harris, Tuesday Mrs Donning – or would another day suit you better? . . . Thank you so much, ladies." I began to see how she controlled the girls so competently. But we did not grudge the loss of one lunch hour, and supervision was easy. It was easy mainly because H3C had not been permitted to join. They were deeply hurt at this at first, and so we eliminated all third forms, "to reduce the numbers" we told them, as sewing machines were limited. They would have been more limited still if H3C had got to work on them, but this explanation was accepted. H3C did not really want to give up any lunch hour to sitting in the clothing room with a teacher but they were sensitive of their bad reputation, and ready to imagine implied insults.

The senior girls made some delightful clothes, and at a special afternoon tea provided by the women staff, a Corso representative accepted their contributions. A press photographer was present, the Headmaster came in for a short while, and the work was displayed on desks round the room. The head girl prefect made a little speech, which she had composed herself and rehearsed for several days. It was not entirely in its original form, as Miss Ferguson had requested that she delete the sentence in which she hoped "that the example of this school will in every way inspire all others." As there were, at that time, three girls suspended, one recently expelled, and two who had just run away from home, I could understand Miss Ferguson's reluctance to have other schools urged to emulate us.

But H3C had done some sewing too. After a few months of teaching them, I wondered whether the vast amount of time which they spent on detentions, and extra work demanded by teachers, could be put to a more constructive use. I suggested to them that, for my punishments at least, they should spend the time in making stuffed rag animals to be given to a children's home. To my surprise, they were enthusiastic about this. We cleared a cupboard and acquired some patterns. H3C brought felt and pieces of material from home (at least, I hoped it was from home and not from some unsuspecting remnant counter), they cut up old rags into little pieces to be used as stuffing, and they provided bright coloured decorations. Helen gave us three bags

237

of rubber chips. As we didn't know until later that she had unpicked two of her mother's best cushions and removed the contents, we thanked her and praised her. Denise's aunt who married a store boss sent along pieces of velvet and yards of ribbon and skeins of coloured wool and silk. We soon had a cupboard full of materials and patterns, and the work began. As a punishment, however, something seemed to be going wrong. The one girl in the class who could ever be called "good" – small earnest Raewyn – came to my room one afternoon in distress when the group was working.

"Why can't I make one too, Mrs Bream?"

"This is a punishment, Raewyn. These girls are staying in after school to do it because they've been naughty."

"Aw let her do one," said Denise. "She's been naughty too. Truly she has."

"She was awful in maths," lied Diane.

"*Were* you, Raewyn?" I asked.

"I *will* be," promised Raewyn solemnly.

Or Heather would come to me with a request for *two* patterns to take home this time, as she had been very bad, not just naughty. I tried to give up the idea that the work was a punishment, but this did not win the class's approval at all. They would willingly stay in at the suggestion that they were to pay the penalty for a misdemeanour; they would come to me and confess the most trivial offences, and demand material; yet it had to have this particular motivation to keep them interested.

Other members of the staff worked in with our scheme, and set "an animal" as an imposition rather than lines or an essay. But much of the work was finished voluntarily at home, and by the end of the year we possessed a hundred and forty-seven animals. There were ducks, pigs, giraffes, rabbits, cats, dogs, zebras, elephants, and many which could never have been found in a natural history book. They were beautifully made, and most appealing. We invited Mr Newall to admire them, which he did most heartily, to the delight of H3C. They were not used to praise and his kind words left them beaming with satisfaction. The fact that each animal represented a crime of some degree, and that the large number of animals only emphasised the misconduct of the class, was now conveniently ignored by us all. We discussed the best way to dispose of the menagerie. Other teachers gave suggestions, complimented H3C, and offered transport to an orphanage. For the first time in the year H3C found themselves in the role of the heroine rather than the villain.

The last weeks of the term passed rapidly, but by this time we were more than normally tired, strained and short-tempered. In the final week I walked into my room one morning feeling worn out and cross. I was not late, I had not been detained, and therefore H3C had had no right to enter the room without permission. Why were they not lined up in the corridor? Moreover, they had sounded even noisier than usual as I had approached the room. And now Lynn had the impertinence to stay out on the floor, instead of going to her seat. And the others were not settling down as usual. I was very annoyed.

"Get to your seat, Lynn," I snapped.

"But Mrs Bream . . . "

"At once!"

Lynn stayed her ground.

"Lynn, do as you're told, you naughty girl." I turned to the rest of the class, who were restless and excited. "I'm just fed up with the bad conduct of you all, and I'm tired of receiving complaints from the other teachers.

When are you going to learn to behave? I'm disgusted with all of you."

"Mrs Bream . . . "

"Be *quiet*, Lynn! You're one of the worst. You are talkative, bad-mannered, and now disobedient. Didn't I tell you to go to your seat? Well what *is* it?"

"Mrs Bream on behalf of the class I would like to thank you for being our form mistress and give you this as a token of appreciation from us all." This carefully prepared and memorised speech was followed by clapping from the class.

Teaching has some very humiliating moments.

Lynn handed me a square package, and I forgot my discomfiture as a worse thought came to me. I knew quite well how H3C acquired the little things they wanted from time to time. Whatever this was, I had no doubt that it was "hot." I opened it in confusion and found a charming little travelling clock. Whatever could I do and say? I could not accept stolen property, yet their intention to reward me was a kind one. But Lynn must have read my thoughts.

"We *bought* it," she announced proudly. "We've got a receipt and all. Each of us put something in and me and Heather and Diane and Denise went down town to choose it. Do you like it?"

So that's where they had been in science yesterday. Mr Hughes had told me they were missing.

"We made Lynn give the speech," said Sally, " 'cos she's good at speeches. Did you think it was a good one?"

By this time I had noticed that the wrapping paper was that used by a well known city department store, and I realised that they had actually done as they said, and bought the gift.

"Do you like it?"

240

"I like it very very much indeed," I told them, "and that was a lovely speech, Lynn." I was ashamed and embarrassed, but H3C had already forgiven me. They always did.

The last days were busy and confused. Desks had to be cleaned, rubbish removed, lockers emptied. Pupils were absent for no accountable reason, but one didn't enquire too closely, as it would have been impossible to keep an accurate check, and the coming holidays promised immunity from punishment.

The final morning was short and disorganised. There were farewells from pupils leaving, magazines to be autographed, cards and gifts from some of the pupils. All were dismissed at eleven a.m. to go home and change into clean uniforms for the afternoon prizegiving.

I went into my room for the last time. Most of H3C were there. They had been busy printing an enormous "Merry Christmas" on the blackboard in red and orange chalk. I wondered briefly from where they had taken the chalk, but this was not the time to enquire.

"You've liked being our form teacher, haven't you?" they asked.

"You're coming back next year, aren't you, Mrs Bream?"

"*Are* you coming back, Mrs Bream?"

"*Are* you?"

I looked at their wicked little faces. I remembered the frustration of that year, the struggles, the headaches, the worry, the futile efforts to teach, the cold days on duty, the daily exhaustion, the nervous strain . . .

"Yes," I promised, "I'll be back."